CROCHET **Jewelry**

CROCHET **Jewelry**

40 beautiful and unique designs

Waejong Kim & Anna Pulvermakher

INTERWEAVE PRESS

A QUARTO BOOK

Copyright © 2007 Quarto Inc.

INTERWEAVE PRESS

Published in North America by

Interweave Press LLC
201 East Fourth Street
Loveland, CO 80537-5655
www.interweave.com
All rights reserved.

Conceived, designed, and produced by
Quarto Publishing plc
The Old Brewery
6 Blundell Street
London N7 9BH

QUA: KNJ

Project editor: Michelle Pickering
Technical editors: Traci Bunkers,
Carol Chambers
Art editor: Natasha Montgomery
Designer: Joelle Wheelwright
Photographer: Simon Pask
Stylist: Thea Lewis
Models: Melissa Milne @ Needhams Models
and Hannah Phaisey @ Sandra Reynolds
Assistant art directors: Penny Cobb,
Caroline Guest

Art director: Moira Clinch
Publisher: Paul Carslake

Color separation by Modern Age Repro
House Ltd, Hong Kong
Printed by SNP Leefung Printers Ltd, China

**Library of Congress
Cataloging-in-Publication Data**
Waejong, Kim.
  Crochet jewelry : 40 beautiful and unique
  designs / Kim Waejong and Anna
  Pulvermakher.
    p. cm.
  Includes index.
  ISBN 978-1-59668-035-7 (pbk.)
  1. Jewelry making. 2. Crocheting--Patterns.
  I. Pulvermakher, Anna. II. Title.
  TT212.W35 2007
  739.27--dc22   2007020355

10 9 8 7 6 5 4 3 2 1

Contents

CHAPTER 4

EARRINGS 90

Snowmen earrings **92**

Hoop earrings **94**

Circle earrings **95**

Denim earrings **96**

Sparkly cross earrings **99**

Ombre earrings **100**

Dangle earrings **101**

Surface crochet earrings **102**

Chandelier drop earrings **103**

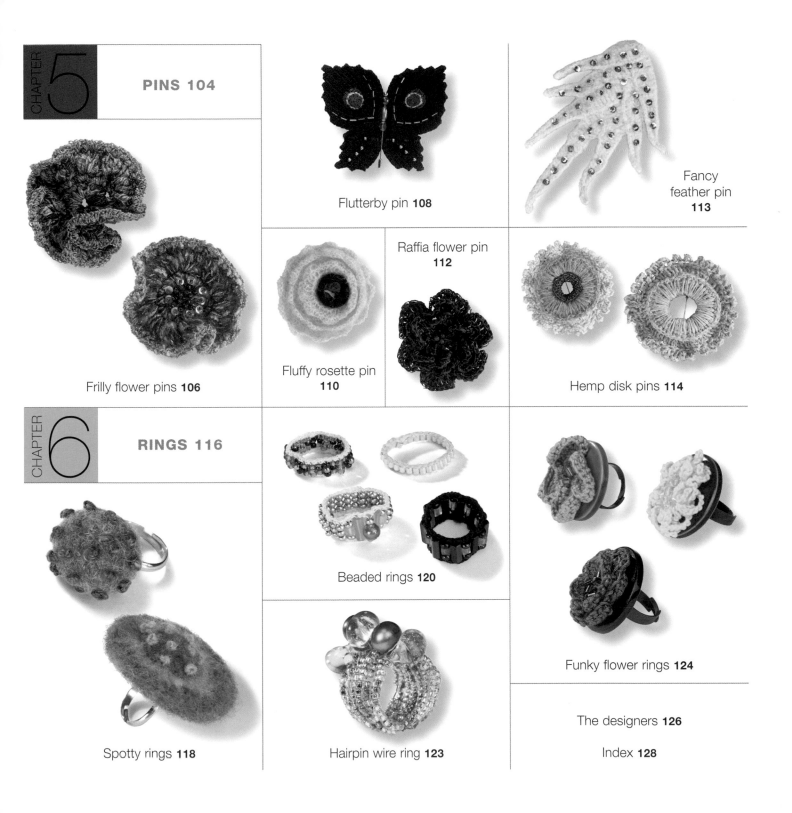

FOREWORD

Crochet has been undergoing a wonderful renaissance in the last several years. Crochet jewelry, in particular, is an amazing phenomenon. Various fashion designers, ranging from Prada to Marc Jacobs, have created beautiful and unique crochet jewelry, and enthusiasts around the world are now exploring the potential of crochet for making jewelry. With a little guidance from this book and a bit of patience, anyone who is familiar with even the most basic crochet stitches can create their own unique crochet jewelry.

This book will teach you how to create gorgeous jewelry made of various yarns, threads, and wire using simple crochet techniques. You can make it more fun by adding all kinds of embellishments and embroidery. Easy-to-follow step-by-step instructions are included. You do not have to be a crochet expert to make this jewelry—anyone can do it. Tools, materials, and techniques are comprehensively discussed at the beginning of the book, providing all the necessary knowledge for you to start working on the projects. Once you master the techniques, you will be able to create amazing handmade pieces for yourself and one-of-a-kind gifts for friends and family. You will cherish these pieces forever and they will never go out of fashion.

With the help of this book, you will be able to bring the wonderful craft of crochet to a new level. Just have fun and use your imagination to its fullest—you will be amazed at the results. Don't be afraid to experiment. You can even combine crochet with knitting, macramé, or embroidery. Try adapting patterns for bigger crochet items, or make miniature pieces by using thinner thread or wire and see what unusual results you can achieve. Featuring projects from an international cast of crochet designers, this book has something to suit everyone's taste. Create anything from snowmen earrings to wonderful flower pins and crochet bead necklaces—the possibilities are virtually limitless.

Waejong Kim & Anna Pulvermakher

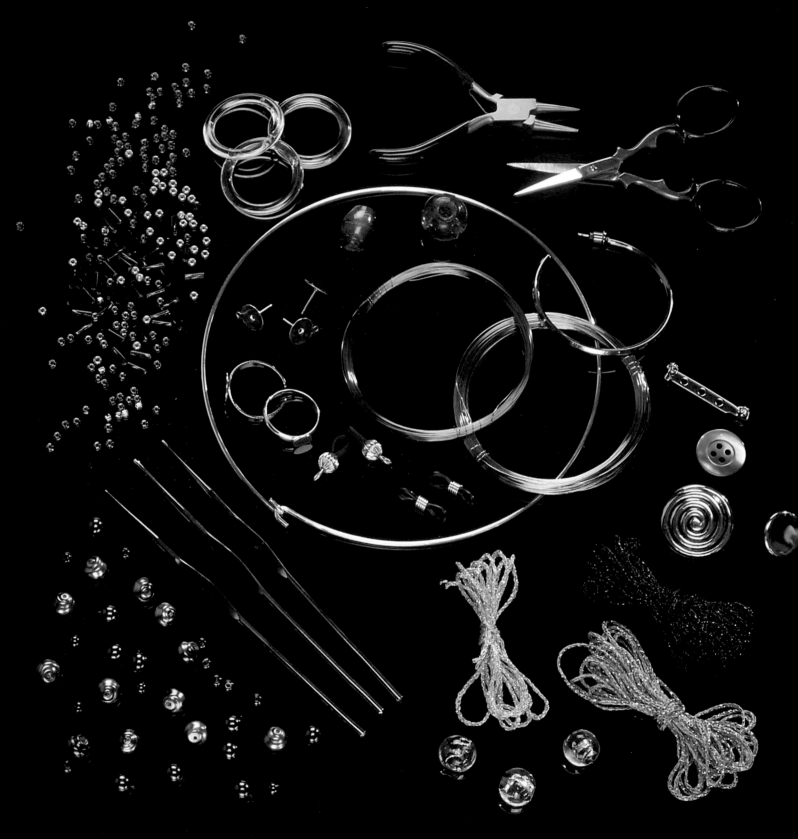

CHAPTER 1

Materials, Tools, and Techniques

This chapter provides an overview of everything you need to make the projects in this book, including materials and tools as well as clear step-by-step instructions on the basic stitches and techniques required. If you are new to crochet, practice them with scrap materials until you feel confident.

YARN, **thread, and wire**

You can crochet with any fine, flexible, continuous material that you can wrap around a crochet hook. There are many different types of yarn, thread, and wire available that are perfect for making crochet jewelry, and because you will only need small amounts, you can use leftover scraps from other projects or splurge on luxury materials that would be too expensive to use on large projects.

Yarn

There is a huge range of yarn available to use for crochet, from very fine cotton to chunky wool. Yarns can be made from one fiber or combine a mixture of two or three different ones in varying proportions. As a general rule, the easiest yarns to use for crochet, especially for a beginner, have a smooth surface and a medium or tight twist.

Woolen yarns and blended yarns with a high proportion of wool feel good to crochet with because they have a certain amount of stretch, making it easy to push the point of the hook into each stitch. Silk yarn has a delightful luster, but it has less resilience than either wool or cotton and is much more expensive. Yarns made from cotton and linen are durable, and may be blended with other fibers to add softness.

Pure wool

Cotton and cotton blends

Yarns made wholly from synthetic fibers, such as acrylic or nylon, are usually less expensive to buy than those made from natural fibers. Yarn is sold by weight, rather than by length, although the packaging of many yarns now includes the length per ball as well as the weight.

Acrylic and acrylic blends

Knitting yarn

Smooth, firm knitting yarns are suitable for crochet. They may be cotton, wool, or synthetic. Special knitting yarns such as silk, glossy viscose, metallic Lurex, and mohair are equally suitable for crochet, but can be more difficult to work with. Knitting yarns are sold in various weights, from superfine to super bulky.

Mohair

Mohair

Silk

Yarn weights	**1**	**2**	**3**	**4**	**5**	**6**
Category	Superfine	Fine	Light	Medium	Bulky	Super bulky
Type of yarns in category	Lace, sock, fingering, baby	Sport, baby	DK, light worsted	Worsted, afghan, aran	Chunky, craft, rug	Bulky, roving
Crochet gauge ranges in single crochet to 4" (10cm)	23–32 sts	16–20 sts	12–17 sts	11–14 sts	8–11 sts	5–9 sts
Recommended hook in metric size range	2.25–3.5mm	3.5–4.5mm	4.5–5.5mm	5.5–6.5mm	6.5–9mm	9mm and larger
Recommended hook in US size range	A–0 to E–4	E–4 to 7	7 to I–9	I–9 to K–10½	K–10½ to M/N–13	M/N–13 and larger

The above reflect the most commonly used gauges and hook sizes for specific yarn categories.

Novelty yarn

Novelty knitting yarns, such as ribbon yarn or blends of mohair and metallic thread, are fun to try and add another dimension to your work. Beware of any yarn that is very heavily textured if the stitch pattern is particularly important to the finished look of the piece, because the patterns made by many stitches will be lost if the yarn is too complex, and it may also be difficult to see the stitch structure when inserting the hook.

Tapestry wool

This pure wool yarn is similar in weight to double knitting (DK) yarn. It is sold in small skeins and a huge range of colors.

Thread

There are numerous types of thread available that can be used for crochet, including cotton thread designed specifically for crochet and the many different types of embroidery thread and floss. Stranded threads can be used as they come from the skein, or separated into individual strands that can then be recombined to create the thickness of thread you require. Skeins need to be wound by hand into balls before you can begin to crochet.

Crochet cotton

Threads sold specifically for crochet are fine, smooth cottons, usually described by a number ranging from 5 (the coarsest) to 60 (very fine yarn used for traditional crochet). These cotton threads are often described as "mercerized," which means they have been treated with an alkali to improve their strength and luster. They are ideal for showing off intricate patterns and textures.

Pearl cotton

Pearl cotton is a firm, twisted thread with a glossy finish, sold for use in crochet, knitting, and embroidery. It gives a softer and less tightly twisted finish than traditional crochet threads. Pearl cotton is manufactured in a range of thicknesses. No. 3 is the heaviest and No. 5 (medium-weight) the most common. Nos. 8 (fine) and 12 (very fine) are also available. This thread may not be divided into strands.

Soft embroidery cotton

A heavyweight, lightly twisted matte thread with a soft, muted appearance.

Cotton embroidery floss (stranded cotton)

A skein is usually formed of six fine strands loosely wound together. Cotton floss is available in hundreds of plain colors, as well as shaded and random-dyed effects.

Synthetic metallic thread

Sometimes called Lurex threads, these were originally developed to imitate true metal threads of real gold and silver. They are available today not just in gold and silver, but also in a wide variety of colors and weights, so a suitable substitute may be found for any weight of thread.

Silk floss

Like cotton floss, this thread may be stranded (four or six strands). The soft sheen of silk adds a touch of luxury to any crochet.

Viscose rayon floss

This floss is an imitation silk thread. It is sometimes tricky to handle, but has a beautiful sheen and depth of color.

Other materials

Don't be afraid to experiment with other materials. Making small pieces of jewelry is the ideal way to test out a new material.

Jewelry wire

The choice of jewelry wire is virtually endless. Most inexpensive wire is plated, which means that the base metal is usually nickel, copper, or aluminum, with a coating to give it the same look as precious metal. Also available are many colored wires. These are coated with either enamel or nylon, and are great for crochet jewelry. However, over long periods of time the color will wear off. Beads can be threaded directly onto the wire without using a needle even when the wire is soft and flexible enough to crochet. Thicker wires are more difficult to crochet than thinner wires. As a general guide, choose wires in the range of 24-gauge (0.5mm) to 32-gauge (0.2mm)—the larger the gauge number, the thinner the wire.

Beading elastic

Fine, medium, and thick beading elastic is available from bead suppliers. They can also be bought from craft and sewing stores.

Hemp, raffia, and other novelty threads

Try crocheting with raffia, hemp, or string (natural or synthetic). Many novelty threads, such as metallic tapes, are sold as embroidery materials and can be used to make wonderful crochet jewelry.

Working with wire

Wire is harder to work with than fiber, so do not use your best tools, and make sure you use an aluminum or steel hook because the wire can damage wood or bamboo ones. When crocheting with wire, you may find it helpful to place the wire in a small drawstring bag, such as an organza gift bag, to help keep it under control and stop if from becoming tangled. If you are new to crocheting with wire, it is a good idea not to spend too much on your first few reels. Then you will not feel quite so bad when discarding sections of wire that have not gone exactly to plan. Do not strive for perfection in your early pieces—it is the overall look that matters.

BEADS **and sequins**

Beads and sequins are great for embellishing crochet jewelry. Whether worked into the fabric during crocheting or sewn on afterward, they always look good. When crocheting with beads or sequins, remember to match the size of the holes in the beads or sequins to the thickness of your yarn.

Seed beads

The term seed bead refers to any small bead. Usually made of glass, seed beads are available in a wide variety of sizes and in many different finishes. The most common type is round, but other shapes are also widely available, including bugle (long cylindrical), cylinder (small cylindrical with extra-large hole), hex (six-sided cylinder), and cube (square with round hole). Whenever the generic term "seed bead" is used in the projects, it is the round seed beads that are being referred to. Seed beads are commonly sold by gram weight.

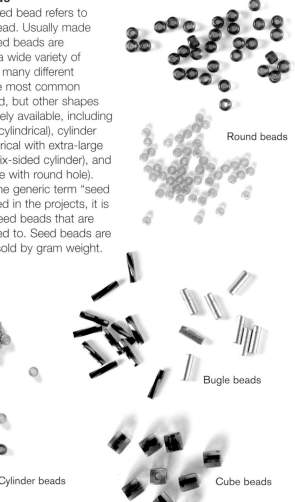

Round beads

Bugle beads

Cylinder beads

Cube beads

Bead finishes

The variety of bead finishes can be bewildering. Here is a handy guide to help you decide which bead you should choose for your project.

AB—Aurora borealis beads have a clear rainbow finish, similar to that seen on oil in water.

Color-lined—The hole through the center of the bead is lined with a different color.

Iris—An iridescent finish is applied to an opaque glass bead, giving it a metallic look.

Luster—A shiny finish that can be clear, colored, or metallic. An opaque lustered bead is called "pearl" and a translucent lustered bead is called "ceylon."

Matte—The glass is etched, giving a soft, frosted finish.

Metallic/galvanized—A metal finish or coating is applied to the bead. Although some of these can last well, this finish can wear off with handling.

Miracle—These Japanese beads have a reflective core that is coated with several layers of colored lacquer. The core reflects light through the lacquer, giving the illusion of depth and a bead within a bead.

Opaque—The glass is a solid color, and light cannot pass through it.

Painted/dyed—Some beads are painted or dyed. Although these beads are beautiful, paint can wear off when the beads are handled or fade in sunlight.

Satin—The glass is striated, giving an effect like the mineral tiger's-eye or satin fabric.

Silver-lined—The hole at the center of the bead has a mirror-like lining, making the bead sparkle.

Other decorative beads

As well as using seed beads, the projects in this book feature a variety of other decorative beads. These include bicone, drop, handblown glass, metal, dichroic glass, Swarovski crystal, wooden, and semiprecious beads. A quick browse through a bead store, catalog, or website will reveal numerous other types—beads in the shape of leaves, flowers, stars, and so on.

Crystal beads

Wooden beads

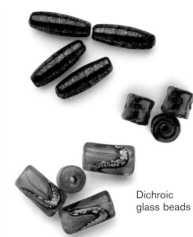

Dichroic glass beads

Handblown glass beads

Metal beads

Sequins

Sequins come in a variety of shapes, sizes, and finishes, and are usually made of plastic. Sequins may be flat or cup-shaped—that is, the edges are faceted and tilt upward. Take care when using the cupped variety that they all face in the same direction (away from the surface of the fabric looks best). As with beads, make sure that the hole in the sequin is large enough to accommodate your yarn if you intend to crochet them into the fabric.

Holographic sequins

Cup sequins

Semiprecious beads

Flower and leaf beads

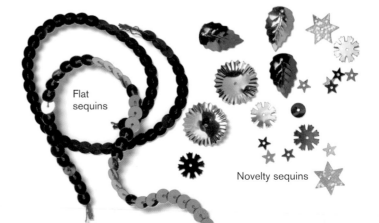

Flat sequins

Novelty sequins

FINDINGS **and notions**

The term findings refers to all the mechanical components used to assemble a piece of jewelry, such as ear wires and clasps. The term notions is used to describe all the small items that you will need in addition to the main materials, such as buttons and beading thread, as well as tools (see pages 22–23).

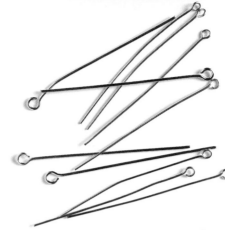

Clasps

There are numerous different types of clasps available, in many shapes, sizes, and finishes. Remember that a good closure can really complement a piece of jewelry. Lobster clasps, shown here, are discrete and tidy, and probably the most useful fastener to have. The lobster clasp is fitted to one end of the finished piece, with a jump ring opposite to fasten it to.

Eye pins and head pins

These are usually used as a support for beads when creating drop earrings. Head pins (right) look like small nails, with the flat head of the pin preventing the beads from falling off. The other end of the pin can be bent into a loop with pliers, ready for attaching other components. Eye pins (above) have a small loop of wire at the head of the pin, from which you can dangle a bead or other component.

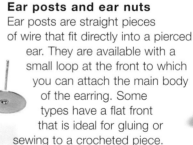

Ear wires

Ear wires are a shepherd's crook shape that slides through a pierced hole in the ear. The main body of the earring is attached to a small loop at the front of the ear wire. Several different styles are available.

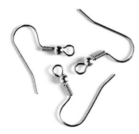

Ear posts and ear nuts

Ear posts are straight pieces of wire that fit directly into a pierced ear. They are available with a small loop at the front to which you can attach the main body of the earring. Some types have a flat front that is ideal for gluing or sewing to a crocheted piece. Ear nuts fit onto the back of ear posts to hold the earrings securely in place.

Jump rings

A jump ring is a metal ring that is not soldered shut so that it can link jewelry components together. Use two pairs of pliers to open the jump ring and to press it shut.

Crimps

Also known as French crimps, these are used to attach fasteners to beading wire and threads. They can also be used simply as beads.

Pin attachments

Pin backs can be sewn onto the back of a finished design that you wish to make into a pin. Hat pins make very decorative attachments.

Ring shanks

Use strong multipurpose glue to attach crochet pieces to ring shanks.

Buttons

Buttons can be used in conjunction with crocheted or beaded loops to fasten items such as necklaces. It is worth searching for an interesting button that will enhance your crochet piece. As with beads, buttons are available in all sorts of materials, shapes, and sizes. Some projects require flat buttons, while others work best with a shank button.

Miscellaneous items

The other items you will need for some of the projects in this book are: glasses keepers, earring and choker hoops, plastic rings, and watch faces and buckles. These are all available from good craft and jewelry stores.

Beading wire

Beading wire is composed of multiple strands of very fine steel cables held together in a plastic or nylon coating. Available in a variety of thicknesses or gauges, it is great for stringing beads and can be used without needles—the beads are simply threaded onto the wire.

Beading thread

Beads can be threaded onto synthetic or natural beading thread and used to add embellishments such as a beaded fringe where a design requires more flexibility than beading wire offers. Consider the weight of the beads and the size of their holes. Choose the strongest thread possible, but remain aware that you want movement in your designs. Beading thread is available in a variety of colors, finishes, and thicknesses. Some types are called bead string. Natural threads are not quite as strong as synthetic threads. For extra security, apply a drop of seam sealant to the ends of threads.

TOOLS **and equipment**

Very little equipment is needed for crochet—all you really need is a hook, although items such as pins and sharp scissors are useful and relatively inexpensive. The tools mentioned here are the basics; others can be bought as you go along.

Aluminum, plastic, bamboo, and resin hooks

Steel hooks

Hooks

Crochet hooks are available in a wide range of sizes, shapes, and materials. The most common types of hooks are made from aluminum or plastic. Small sizes of steel hooks are made for working crochet with very fine cotton (often called thread crochet). Some brands of aluminum and steel hooks have plastic handles to give a better grip (often called "soft touch" handles) and make the work easier on the fingers. Handmade wooden and horn hooks are also available, many featuring decorative handles. Bamboo hooks are great to work with because they are made from a natural material and have a very smooth finish.

Choosing a hook is largely a matter of personal preference, and will depend on various factors such as hand size and weight of hook. The most important things to consider when choosing a hook is how it feels in your hand and the ease with which it works with your yarn. When you have found your perfect brand of hook, it is useful to buy several different sizes. Store your hooks in a clean container—you can buy a fabric roll with loops to secure the hooks, or use a zippered pouch such as a cosmetic bag.

Hook sizes

Crochet hooks come in a range of sizes, from very thick to very fine, to suit different yarn weights. Finer yarns usually require a smaller hook, thicker yarns a larger hook. Hooks from different manufacturers, and those made from different materials, can vary widely in size even though they may all be branded with the same number or letter to indicate their size. In addition, hook sizes are quoted differently in the United States and Europe, and some brands of hooks are labeled with more than one type of numbering. Many US manufacturers are now labeling hooks more prominently with metric sizing, which should lead to greater standardization.

Aluminum hooks			Steel hooks		
US	Metric (mm)	UK	US	Metric (mm)	UK
A–0	2.0	14	00	3.5	–
B–1	2.25	13	0	3.25	0
–	2.5	12	1	2.75	1
C–2	2.75	–	2	2.25	1½
D–3	3.25	10	3	2.1	2
E–4	3.5	9	4	2.0	2½
F–5	3.75	–	5	1.9	3
G–6	4.0	8	6	1.8	3½
7	4.5	7	7	1.65	4
H–8	5.0	6	8	1.5	4½
I–9	5.5	5	9	1.4	5
J–10	6.0	4	10	1.3	5½
K–10½	6.5	3	11	1.1	6
–	7.0	2	12	1.0	6½
L–11	8.0	0	13	0.85	7
M/N–13	9.0	00	14	0.75	–
N/P–15	10	000			
P/Q	15	–			
Q	16	–			
S	19	–			

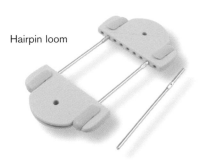

Hairpin loom

Markers

Glass-headed pins

Quilters' pins

Hairpin loom

Hairpin looms are adjustable, so you can make different widths of crochet. The metal pins are held in position by clips or bars at the top and bottom, and they can be placed close together to make a narrow strip or moved farther apart to make a wide strip.

Markers

Split rings or shaped loops made from brightly colored plastic can be slipped onto your crochet to mark a place on a pattern, to indicate the beginning row of a repeat, and to help with counting the stitches on the foundation chain.

Sewing needles

Tapestry needles have blunt points and long eyes and are normally used for counted thread embroidery. They come in a range of sizes and are used for weaving in yarn ends and for sewing pieces of crochet together. Very large blunt-ended needles are often labeled as "yarn needles." You may also need a selection of sewing needles with sharp points for applying sequins, working embroidery stitches, and so on.

Pins

Glass-headed rustproof pins are the best type to use for blocking (see page 44). Plastic-headed or pearl-headed pins can be used for pinning crochet and for cold-water blocking, but do not use this type for steam blocking because the heat of the iron will melt the plastic heads. Quilters' long pins with fancy heads are useful when pinning pieces of crochet together because the heads are easy to see and will not slip through the crochet fabric.

Beading needles

Beading needles are available in both long and short lengths as well as in different thicknesses. The size you use will be determined by the size of the beads and the type of thread or wire. As a general guide, size 10 needles are suitable for most beaded projects. Twisted wire beading needles are made from twisted wire with a loop at one end; they are useful when working with very small beads or when you need to take the thread or wire through the same beads several times. Very fine "Big Eye" needles are split by an "eye" that runs right down the center of the needle, making them very easy to thread.

Tape measure

Choose one that shows both inches and centimeters on the same side and replace it when it becomes worn or frayed because this means it will probably have stretched and become inaccurate. A 12" (30cm) metal or plastic ruler is also useful for measuring gauge swatches.

Sharp scissors

Choose a small, pointed pair to cut yarn and trim off yarn ends.

Wire cutters and pliers

Use a pair of wire cutters for cutting wire and trimming metal findings, and at least one pair of pliers for bending wire. Two pairs would be ideal, such as a pair of flat-nose pliers and a pair of round-nose pliers.

Wire cutters

Flat-nose pliers

Round-nose pliers

Sewing needles

Beading needles

GETTING **started**

The first step when beginning to crochet is to create a foundation chain of loops. It is also important to hold the hook and yarn correctly. There are many ways of doing this; the best method is the one that feels comfortable to you.

Holding the hook

There are a few different methods of holding the hook and yarn. There is no right or wrong way. The most important thing is to use the method that you prefer and the type of hook that you find most comfortable.

Holding the yarn

It is important to wrap the yarn around your fingers to control the supply of yarn and to keep the gauge even. You can hold the yarn in several ways, but again it is best to use the method that feels the most comfortable.

Making a slipknot

All crochet is made up from one loop on the hook at any time. The first working loop begins as a slipknot and does not count as a stitch.

1 Take the short end of the yarn in one hand—about 6" (15cm)—and wrap it around the forefinger of your other hand.

Pen hold
Hold the hook as if it were a pen, with the tips of your thumb and forefinger over the flat section or middle of the hook.

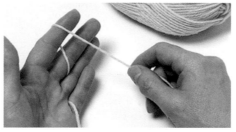

1 Loop the short end of the yarn over your forefinger, with the yarn coming from the ball under the next finger. Grip the length of yarn coming from the ball gently with your third and little fingers.

2 Slip the loop off your forefinger and push a loop of the short end of the yarn through the loop from your forefinger.

Knife hold
Hold the hook as if it were a knife, almost grasping the flat section or middle of the hook between your thumb and forefinger.

2 Alternatively, loop the short end of the yarn over your forefinger, with the yarn coming from the ball under your next two fingers and then wrapped around the little finger.

3 Insert the hook into this second loop. Gently pull the short end of the yarn to tighten the loop around the hook and complete the slipknot.

Working a foundation chain (ch)

From the slipknot, you can now create a foundation chain (this is similar to casting on in knitting).

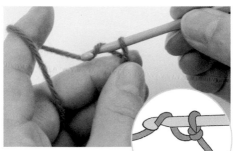

1 Hold the hook with the slipknot in one hand. With your other hand, grip the shorter piece of yarn just under the slipknot with your thumb and middle finger, and hold the longer piece of yarn over the forefinger. To create the first chain stitch, use your forefinger to wrap the yarn over the hook (known as "yarn over").

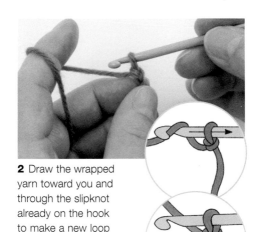

2 Draw the wrapped yarn toward you and through the slipknot already on the hook to make a new loop and complete the chain stitch.

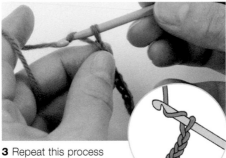

3 Repeat this process until the chain is the required length. Move your thumb and middle finger up the chain as it lengthens to keep the gauge even.

Counting chains

The front of the chain looks like a series of V shapes, while the back of the chain forms a distinctive "bump" of yarn behind each V shape. When counting chain stitches, count each V shape on the front of the chain as one chain stitch, except for the chain stitch on the hook (the working stitch), which is not counted. You may find it easier to turn the chain over and count the "bumps" on the back of the chain.

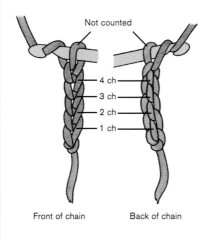

Not counted

4 ch
3 ch
2 ch
1 ch

Front of chain   Back of chain

Working into a foundation chain

The first row of stitches is worked into the foundation chain. There are two ways of doing this, with the first method being easiest for a beginner.

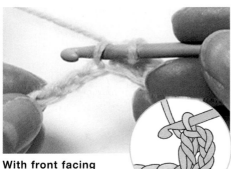

With front facing
Hold the chain with the front (V shapes) facing you. Insert the hook into the top loop of each chain stitch. This gives a loose edge to a piece of crochet.

With back facing
Hold the chain with the back ("bumps") facing you. Insert the hook into the "bump" at the back of each chain stitch. This makes a stronger, neater edge.

Use markers to help when counting a long foundation chain, placing a marker every 10 to 20 chain stitches.

BASIC stitches

Various stitches can be worked onto the foundation chain to form a crochet fabric. Each stitch gives a different texture and varies in depth.

Turning chains

When working crochet either in rows or rounds, you need to work a specific number of extra chain stitches at the beginning of each row or round. These stitches are called a turning chain when worked at the beginning of a straight row and a beginning chain when worked at the beginning of a round. What they do is bring the hook up to the correct height for the next stitch to be worked, so the longer the stitch, the longer the turning chain that is necessary.

The list below shows the standard number of chain stitches needed to make a turn for each type of basic crochet stitch, but a pattern may vary from this in order to produce a specific effect. If you have a tendency to work chain stitches very tightly, you may need to work an extra chain stitch in order to keep the edges of your work from becoming too tight.

Number of turning chain stitches
• Single crochet = 1 turning chain
• Half double crochet = 2 turning chains
• Double crochet = 3 turning chains
• Treble crochet = 4 turning chains

Counting turning chain stitches

The turning or beginning chain is counted as the first stitch of the row or round except when working single crochet, when the turning chain is ignored. For example, ch 4 (counts as 1 tr) at the beginning of a row or round means that the turning or beginning chain contains four chain stitches, and these are counted as the equivalent of one treble crochet stitch. A turning or beginning chain may be longer than the number required for the stitch, and in that case counts as one stitch plus a number of chains. For example, ch 6 (counts as 1 tr, ch 2) means that the turning or beginning chain is the equivalent of one treble crochet stitch plus two chain stitches.

At the end of the row or round, the final stitch is usually worked into the turning or beginning chain of the previous row or round. The final stitch may be worked into the top chain stitch of the turning or beginning chain or into another specified stitch of the chain. For example, 1 dc into third of ch 3 means that the final stitch is a double crochet stitch and it is worked into the third stitch of the turning or beginning chain.

Single crochet

Slip stitch (sl st)

This is commonly used to join ends of work together to form a ring, to join a round, or to move the hook and yarn across a group of existing stitches to a new position. To work a slip stitch, insert the hook from front to back into the second chain from the hook or the indicated stitch. Wrap the yarn over the hook, then draw the yarn toward you through both the chain or stitch and the loop on the hook. Continue working slip stitches in each chain along the row or as indicated in the pattern.

Single crochet (sc)

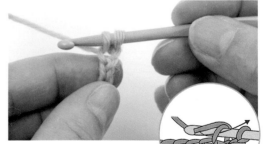

1 Work the foundation chain plus one extra chain stitch (this is the turning chain). Insert the hook from front to back into the second chain from the hook. Wrap the yarn over the hook and draw the yarn through the chain toward you, leaving two loops on the hook.

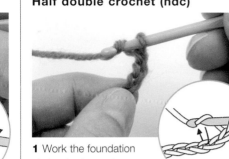

Half double crochet (hdc)

2 To complete the stitch, wrap the yarn over the hook again and draw it through both loops on the hook, leaving one loop on the hook.

1 Work the foundation chain plus two extra chain stitches (this is the turning chain). Wrap the yarn over the hook, then insert the hook from front to back into the third chain from the hook.

4 Continue in this way along the row, working one half double crochet into each chain stitch. At the end of the row, turn the work.

3 Continue in this way along the row, working one single crochet stitch into each chain stitch. At the end of the row, turn the work.

2 Wrap yarn over the hook again and draw the yarn through the chain toward you, leaving three loops on the hook.

5 When working back along the row, work two chain stitches for the turning chain, which counts as the first half double crochet. Skip the first half double crochet stitch at the beginning of the row, then insert the hook from front to back under both loops of each remaining half double crochet stitch of the previous row. At the end of the row, work the last stitch into the top stitch of the turning chain.

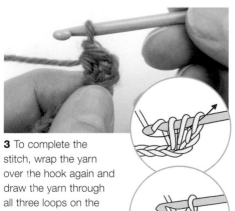

4 When working back along the row, work one chain stitch for the turning chain. Then insert the hook from front to back under both loops of the single crochet stitches of the previous row. Work the final single crochet stitch into the last stitch of the row below, not into the turning chain.

3 To complete the stitch, wrap the yarn over the hook again and draw the yarn through all three loops on the hook, leaving one loop on the hook.

Half double crochet

Double crochet (dc)

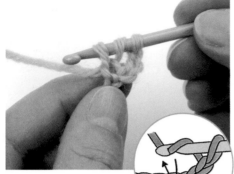

1 Work the foundation chain plus three extra chain stitches (this is the turning chain). Wrap the yarn over the hook, then insert the hook from front to back into the fourth chain from the hook. Wrap the yarn over the hook again and draw the yarn through the chain toward you, leaving three loops on the hook.

2 Wrap the yarn over the hook again and draw it through the first two loops, leaving two loops on the hook.

3 To complete the stitch, wrap the yarn over the hook again and draw it through the last two loops, leaving one loop on the hook.

4 Continue in this way along the row, working one double crochet stitch into each chain stitch. At the end of the row, turn the work.

5 When working back along the row, work three chain stitches for the turning chain, which counts as the first double crochet. Skip the first double crochet stitch at the beginning of the row and insert the hook from front to back though both loops of each remaining double crochet stitch of the previous row. At the end of the row, work the last stitch into the top of the turning chain.

Working into front and back of stitches

It is usual to work crochet stitches under both loops of the stitches made on the previous row. However, sometimes a pattern will instruct you to work under just one loop, either the back or the front, in which case the remaining loop becomes a horizontal ridge. When using either method with a plain piece of double crochet, the edges of the fabric may become stretchy. To prevent this, try working into both loops of the first and last stitches on every row.

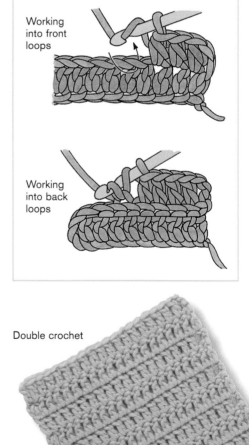

Working into front loops

Working into back loops

Double crochet

Treble (or triple) crochet (tr)

1 Work the foundation chain plus four extra chain stitches (this is the turning chain). Wrap the yarn over the hook twice, then insert the hook from front to back into the fifth chain from the hook. Wrap the yarn over the hook again and draw the yarn through the chain toward you, leaving four loops on the hook.

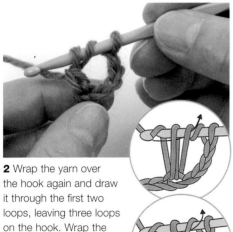

2 Wrap the yarn over the hook again and draw it through the first two loops, leaving three loops on the hook. Wrap the yarn over the hook again and draw it through the first two loops, leaving two loops on the hook.

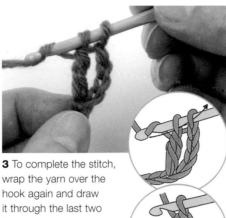

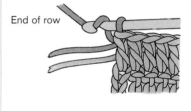

3 To complete the stitch, wrap the yarn over the hook again and draw it through the last two loops, leaving one loop on the hook.

4 Continue in this way along the row, working one treble crochet into each chain stitch. At the end of the row, turn the work. When working back along the row, work four chains for the turning chain, which counts as the first treble crochet. Skip the first treble crochet stitch at the beginning of the row, then insert the hook from front to back through both loops of each remaining treble crochet stitch of the previous row. At the end of the row, work the last stitch into the top of the turning chain.

Joining a new yarn or color

Whether you are joining a new ball of yarn or a new color, the method is the same. It is best to join a new yarn at the end of a row, but you can join it anywhere in a row if you need to. Leave the last stage of the final stitch incomplete, loop the new yarn around the hook, and use it to complete the stitch. Work the next row in the new yarn or color as required. When changing color in the middle of a row, begin the stitch in the usual way, wrap the new yarn over the hook, draw the new yarn through the stitch toward you, and then work the stitch.

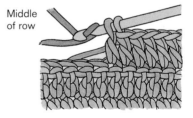

End of row

Middle of row

Treble crochet

WORKING **in rounds**

Some circular pieces of crochet require that you work in rounds rather than rows. The basic stitch techniques are the same, but you work around the crochet rather than back and forth in straight rows.

Making a foundation ring

1 To start, you have to make a ring by joining a small length of chain with a slip stitch. The chain is usually between four and six stitches, depending on the thickness of yarn being used.

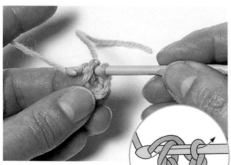

2 Insert the hook from front to back through the first chain made. Wrap the yarn over the hook and draw it toward you through the chain and loop on the hook, as if working a slip stitch.

3 Gently tighten the first stitch by pulling the loose yarn end. You have now created a ring of chains.

Working into the ring

1 The foundation ring is the center of your circular crochet and where you will work into on the next round. Depending on the stitch you will be using, make the appropriate length of beginning chain.

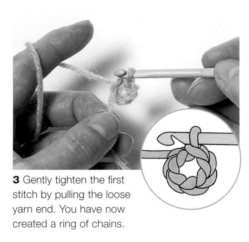

2 Insert the hook from front to back into the center of the ring (not into the chain) for each stitch and work the number of stitches specified in the pattern. When working in rounds, the right side is always facing you unless the instructions indicate to turn at the end of a round.

3 When you have worked around the full circle, finish off the round by working a slip stitch into the top of the beginning chain worked at the beginning of the round. Continue working in rounds to build up the pattern, working into each stitch of the previous round in the usual way and joining the end of each round with a slip stitch.

Fastening off the final round

For a really neat edge on the final round, use this method of sewing the first and last stitches together in preference to the slip-stitch method shown opposite.

1 Cut the yarn, leaving an end of about 4" (10cm), and draw it though the last stitch. With right side facing, thread the end in a tapestry needle and take it under both loops of the stitch next to the beginning chain.

2 Pull the needle through, then insert it into the center of the last stitch of the round. On the wrong side, pull the needle through to complete the stitch, adjust the length of the stitch to close the round, then weave in the end on the wrong side in the usual way.

Tubular crochet

Tubular crochet is worked in the round to form a cylinder, which can be as wide or narrow as you wish. There are several methods of working tubular crochet. In this book, rounds of single crochet stitches are worked without making a join; this forms a tube with a spiral pattern.

1 Make the required length of chain and join it with a slip stitch to form a ring. Turn and work one row of single crochet into the chain (not into the ring). Join the round by working a single crochet into the first stitch.

2 Insert a marker into the single crochet just worked to mark the beginning of a new round. Continue the new round, working a single crochet into each stitch of the previous round.

3 When you reach the marker, do not join the round. Instead, remove the marker and work the marked stitch.

4 Replace the marker in the new stitch to mark the start of the new round. Continue working around and around, moving the marker each time you reach it, until the cylinder is the required length. Fasten off.

Single crochet tube

SHAPING **techniques**

Shaping your crochet is done by increasing or decreasing stitches. When adding or subtracting stitches at intervals along a row, this is called internal increase or decrease. When adding or subtracting stitches at the beginning or end of a row, this is called external increase or decrease. Each method creates a different effect.

External increases

This method involves adding extra foundation chains at the beginning or end of a row.

At beginning of row
1 To add stitches at the beginning of a row, work the required number of extra chains at the end of the previous row and remember to add the turning chains.

2 On the next row, work the extra stitches along the chain and then continue along the row.

At end of row
1 To add stitches at the end of a row, leave the last few stitches of the row unworked. Remove the hook and join a length of yarn to the last stitch of the row and work the required number of extra foundation chains (a different color is used here for clarity). Fasten off the yarn.

2 Place the hook back into the row, complete the row, and then continue working extra stitches across the chain.

Internal increases

This is the simplest method of adding stitches at intervals along a row. Working internal increases one stitch in from the edge is often used to shape garment edges neatly.

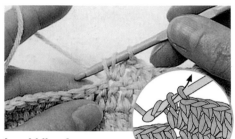

In middle of row
Work to the point where you want to increase, then work two or more stitches into one stitch on the previous row.

At beginning of row
At the beginning of the row, work the first stitch and then work the increase as described above.

At end of row
At the end of the row, work to the last two stitches, work the increase in the next to last stitch, and then work the last stitch.

Internal decreases

This method involves skipping stitches or working two or more stitches together. As with the internal increases, work the decrease one stitch in from the edge for a neat finish.

Skipping a stitch

The easiest way to decrease one stitch is simply to skip one stitch of the previous row.

Sc2tog

To work two stitches together in single crochet, start working the first stitch of the decrease but do not complete it; instead, leave two loops on the hook. Insert the hook into the next stitch and work another incomplete stitch so that you have three loops on the hook. Wrap the yarn over the hook and draw it through all three loops on the hook.

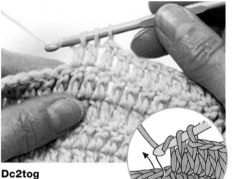

Dc2tog

To work two stitches together in double crochet, start working the first stitch of the decrease but do not complete it; instead, leave two loops on the hook. Insert the hook into the next stitch and work another incomplete stitch so that you have three loops on the hook. Wrap the yarn over the hook and draw it through all three loops on the hook.

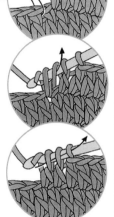

Internal increases and decreases are used one stitch in from the beginning and end of rows to produce a chevron shape.

External decreases

This method is best used if you want to decrease several stitches at one time.

At beginning of row

To decrease at the beginning of a row, work a slip stitch into each of the stitches that you want to decrease, then work the turning chain and continue along the row.

At end of row

To decrease at the end of a row, leave the stitches to be decreased unworked. Work the turning chain, then turn and work along the next row.

External increases and decreases are used to add or subtract groups of stitches at the beginning and end of rows produce a cross shape.

OTHER STITCH **techniques**

Having learned the basic stitches, you will find that there are many variations on how they can be combined and adapted to create specific effects.

Raised stitches

Stitches made with this technique are known by several different names: raised stitches, post stitches, or relief stitches. They create a heavily textured surface, made by inserting the hook around the post (stem) of the stitches on the previous row, and then working a stitch. The hook can be inserted from the front or the back of the work, giving a different effect each way. When working a front post stitch, insert the hook into the front of the fabric, around the back of the post, and return to the front of the work. When working a back post stitch, insert the hook from the back of the fabric, around the front of the post, and out through to the back of the work.

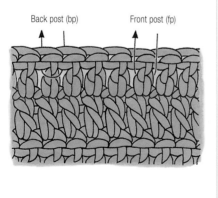

Back post (bp)   Front post (fp)

Lacework

Lacework is light, pretty, and delicate to look at when worked in lightweight yarns.

Changing the hook position

Working in slip stitch across one or more stitches is a useful way of changing the position of the yarn and hook. Pattern directions may refer to this as "slip stitch across" or "slip stitch into." Here, slip stitches are being worked into the edge of a petal in order to move the hook and yarn from the valley between two petals to the tip of one petal, ready to work the next stitches of the pattern.

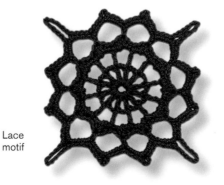

Lace motif

Chain spaces

Long strands of chain stitches, described as chain spaces, chain loops, or chain arches, are an integral part of lacework. They are sometimes used as a foundation for stitches worked in the following row or round, or they may form a visible part of the design.

1 Work chain spaces as evenly as possible, anchoring them by working a slip stitch or single crochet into the previous row or round.

2 When a chain space is worked as a foundation on one row, stitches are worked over the chains on the following row. To do this, simply insert the hook into the space below the strand of chain stitches to work each stitch, not directly into individual chain stitches.

Shell pattern

Shell patterns are formed from three or more stitches that share the same chain, stitch, or chain space, resulting in a triangular group of stitches that looks like a clam shell. Usually, chains or stitches at either side of a shell are skipped to compensate for the shell, and each stitch making up a shell is counted as one stitch. Large groups of stitches formed into shells are known as fan stitches.

Spike stitches

Spike stitches (also called dropped stitches) are worked over the top of other stitches to add color or texture to crochet. The stitches are worked singly or in groups over one or more rows and are usually worked in single crochet. As well as making interesting color patterns when worked in two or more contrasting colors, spike stitches also create a thick, densely worked, padded fabric.

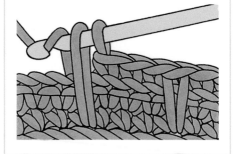

Crocheted loop fasteners

Button loops can be created by working a loop of chains large enough to accommodate the button. Work to the position of the loop, or attach a new length of yarn.

1 Work a length of chain stitches long enough to fit around the button being used. Remember that the loop will stretch slightly, so make it on the small side.

2 Slip the hook out of the chain and insert it into the crochet at the point where you want the loop to finish. Insert the hook into the last chain of the loop, wrap the yarn over the hook, and join the loop to the crochet with a slip stitch. You can reinforce the loop if you wish by working single crochet stitches around it until the chain is completely covered.

Picot edging

Picot is a delicately toothed edge on a piece of crochet. It is formed by three or more chain stitches closed into a ring with a slip stitch or single crochet stitch. Work the number of chains required, then insert the hook as instructed in the pattern. The instruction may either be to insert the hook into the back of the first chain stitch of the picot and work a slip stitch into it, or to insert the hook down through the top of the previous single crochet stitch and work a slip stitch into it. Skip the next stitch along the edge of the piece, then work a slip stitch into the following stitch.

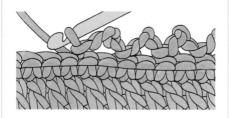

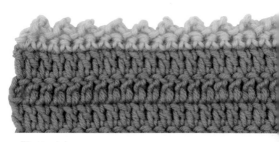

Picot edging

Shell edging

Surface crochet

Surface crochet is exactly as the name suggests—crochet worked on top of a crochet background. It is easier to work surface crochet on an open mesh background, but you can work it on more compact stitch backgrounds as well.

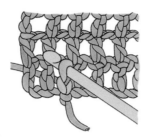

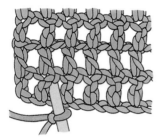

1 Make a slipknot in the surface crochet yarn and slip it onto the hook. Insert the hook through a hole in the background fabric in the required position.

2 Holding the surface crochet yarn behind the background fabric, wrap the yarn over the hook and draw it through the fabric and through the loop on the hook to make a slip stitch. For beaded surface crochet, simply bring the required number of beads through to the surface of the background fabric for each slip stitch.

3 Continue working surface crochet as instructed in the pattern. When you have finished, break the yarn and pull it through the last stitch to secure.

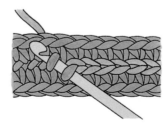

4 When using a compact fabric, such as single or half double crochet, take care not to work the background stitches too tightly.

Surface crochet worked in mohair and metallic yarns.

Crocheted cords

Crocheted cords make attractive ties to secure a necklace or other crochet jewelry. Single crochet cords are featured in the projects in this book.

1 Work a foundation chain to the required length. Insert the hook into the second chain from the hook and work a row of single crochet stitches along one side of the chain.

2 At the end of the first side, work three single crochet stitches in the last stitch to curve around the corner, then work along the other side of the chain, working into the unused loops of the foundation chain in single crochet as before. Work two single crochet in the last stitch and join with a slip stitch to the first single crochet.

Single crochet cord

Single crochet cord with surface crochet stripe

Crocheted buttons

Choosing an attractive button can be very important to the look of a piece of jewelry. Try crocheting around a bead or small ball of batting of the required size. See page 51 for an alternative method of crocheting around a bead.

1 Using a smaller hook than suggested for the yarn you are using, ch 2, then work 4 sc into the first ch. Without joining or turning the work, work 2 sc into each stitch made on the previous round. For every following increase round, work *1 sc into first st, 2 sc into next stitch; repeat from * until the piece covers one half of the bead or ball of batting.

2 Slip the bead or ball into the crochet cover. Start decreasing by working *1 sc into next st, then sc2tog; repeat from * until the bead or ball of batting is completely covered.

3 Break off the yarn, leaving an end about 12" (30cm) long. Thread the yarn into a tapestry needle and work a few stitches to secure. Either fasten off the end of yarn in the usual way or use it to attach the crocheted button to another item.

Crocheting around hoops or rings

Crocheting around plastic rings, choker hoops, or earring hoops is a great way to make your own unique jewelry.

Without a chain

Starting with a slipknot on the hook, work a round of single crochet stitches over the ring or hoop. Do this by inserting the hook through the middle of the ring or hoop in the same way as you would work into a foundation ring of chain stitches when working in the round (see page 30). Continue until the ring or hoop is completely covered, or as instructed in the pattern.

Single crochet button

With a chain—hoop single crochet (hsc)

1 Work a chain as instructed in the pattern. Hold the hoop in front of the chain. *Insert the hook in front of the hoop through the hump of the next chain. Yo (at back of the hoop), then pull through the loop to the front.

2 Yo, then pull through two loops over the hoop to form a stitch around the hoop. Repeat from * to work each hsc as instructed in the pattern.

BEADED **crochet**

Beads can be applied to crochet at the same time as the stitches are being worked, or they can be sewn on afterward (see page 107). When working the beads into the fabric, you need to thread all the beads onto the yarn before starting to crochet, making sure they are in the correct sequence. You can use exactly the same techniques with sequins as well.

Sequinned single crochet

Beaded single crochet

Threading the beads

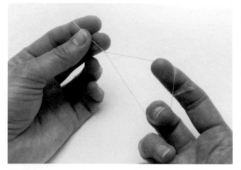

1 Thread a sewing or beading needle with thread and knot the ends to form a loop.

2 Pass the end of the yarn through the loop. Thread the beads onto the needle, then push them down over the thread and onto the yarn. Make sure you thread the beads in the correct sequence.

Beaded chain (bch)

Make a slipknot in the usual way, then push a bead up the yarn to sit just under the hook. Wrap the yarn over the hook. Pull the yarn through the knot, leaving the bead at the front of the work, lying on the chain. Continue in this way for each beaded chain stitch required in the pattern. You can place more than one bead at a time using the same technique. When placing large beads, you may need to work extra chain stitches between beads to allow for their size.

Beaded single crochet (bsc)

When indicated in the pattern, push a bead up the yarn to sit just under the crochet hook. Keeping the bead in position, insert the hook into the next stitch and draw the yarn through so that there are two loops on the hook. Wrap the yarn over the hook again and draw it through to complete the single crochet stitch. Continue adding beads in this way, following the pattern instructions. You can place more than one bead at a time using this technique.

Beading sequence

When working with beads that need to be arranged in a particular pattern, make sure that you thread the different beads onto the yarn in reverse order, so the pattern will work out correctly as you crochet. The instructions for the projects in this book list the sequence for threading beads.

WIRE **crochet**

Crocheting with wire is exactly the same as crocheting with yarn, but is harder on the fingers. Work slowly to avoid making mistakes, because raveling stitches will reduce the workability of the wire and may cause it to break; the appearance of the wire may also be spoiled. Beaded chain is shown here, but any crochet stitch can be worked with wire.

Beaded chain (bch)

1 Thread the beads onto the wire. Twist the wire to form a loop and place it on the hook.

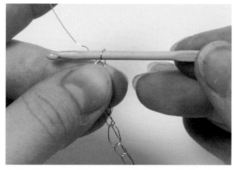

3 Continue working chain stitches until the chain reaches the required length.

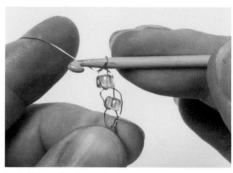

5 Pull the wire through the loop on the hook, making sure that the bead sits neatly on the chain. Continue working beaded chain stitches in this way until the required length is achieved. Practice working single crochet and beaded single crochet as well.

Gently "tweak" the stitches to make sure each bead is sitting within each chain link.

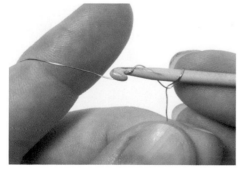

2 Holding the short end of the wire firmly between the thumb and middle finger of your left hand, wrap the wire over the hook and then draw the wrapped wire through the slipknot to complete the first chain stitch.

4 To work a beaded chain stitch, slide a bead up the wire until it sits just under the hook, close to the last chain stitch. Wrap the wire over the hook.

HAIRPIN **crochet**

Hairpin crochet (also called hairpin lace and hairpin braid) is worked with a hairpin loom. A crochet hook is used to form a series of loops between the two pins on the loom, producing a strip of very lacy crochet.

Working a basic strip

1 Arrange the pins in the bottom clip so they are the required distance apart. Make a slipknot in the yarn and loop it over the left-hand pin.

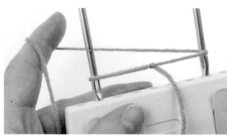

2 Ease the knot across so it lies in the center between the pins. Take the yarn back around the right-hand pin, tensioning it between your fingers as if you were working ordinary crochet.

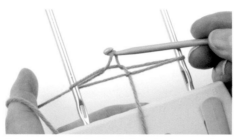

3 Insert the crochet hook into the loop on the left-hand pin, wrap the yarn over the hook, and draw it through the loop.

4 Wrap the yarn over the hook again and draw it through the loop on the hook to secure the yarn. This completes the first single crochet stitch.

Hairpin crochet strip

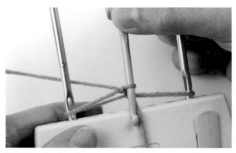

5 Twist the hook around so that the handle points upward and is above the work, then take hold of the handle through the pins from the back of the loom. Turn the loom 180 degrees clockwise to make a half turn, allowing the yarn to wind around the right-hand pin as you do so. The other side of the clip will be facing you, and you will be holding the hook in front of the loom.

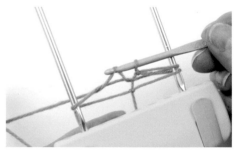

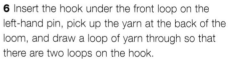

6 Insert the hook under the front loop on the left-hand pin, pick up the yarn at the back of the loom, and draw a loop of yarn through so that there are two loops on the hook.

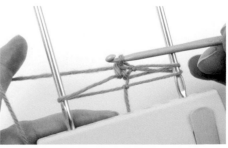

7 Wrap the yarn over the hook and draw it through the two loops on the hook to make a single crochet stitch.

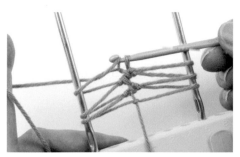

8 Repeat steps 5, 6, and 7 until the hairpin loom is filled with braid, remembering to turn the loom clockwise each time. When following pattern instructions that specify working a number of loops, count the loops on both pins.

9 When the loom is full, put the top clip onto the pins, remove the lower clip, and slide the crochet strip downward, leaving the last few loops on the pins.

10 Reinsert the lower clip, remove the top clip, and continue working the strip as above. When the strip is the required length, pull the yarn end through the last stitch with the hook, and slide the strip off the pins.

Incorporating beads

Beads can be incorporated into the loops as well as the central stitches of the hairpin strip. Thread the beads onto the wire in the correct sequence (the last beads threaded onto the wire will be the first beads used). Here, groups of small seed beads are incorporated into each loop, with a single larger bead in each stitch. This example uses wire, but you can incorporate beads into a yarn strip in the same way.

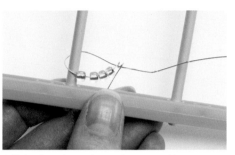

1 Twist the wire to form a loop, catching the required number of beads in the loop. Slip the loop onto the left-hand pin of the loom. If using yarn, start with a slipknot in the usual way, but make sure you catch the beads in the loop part of the slipknot.

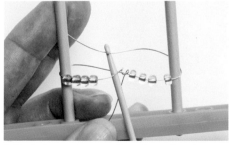

2 Push the next group of beads up the wire, then wrap the wire around the right-hand pin of the loom. Insert the crochet hook into the loop on the left-hand pin, wrap the wire over the hook, and draw it through the loop.

3 Push the first larger bead up to the hook, then wrap the wire over the hook again and draw it through the loop on the hook to complete the first beaded single crochet stitch.

4 Catching more seed beads in the loop as required, turn the loom 180 degrees in the usual way, but remove the hook from the stitch as you do so to avoid overworking the wire. Continue working the hairpin strip, catching beads in the loops and stitches as required.

Using guidelines

Joining and edging hairpin strips can be a little awkward because the loops have a natural twist to them, making it difficult to distinguish the front and back of each loop. After working the first two loops, thread a length of scrap yarn through them and tie it to the top of the clip of the loom to form a U shape. Make sure you work subsequent loops around the guidelines.

CABLE **techniques**

You can use hairpin crochet as it comes off the loom, or you can join pieces together. There are several different methods of doing this, but the projects in this book use a 1x1 and 2x2 cable join. You can also apply a decorative edging, such as a cable heading.

Cable join

A cable join involves slip-stitching the loops of two strips of hairpin crochet through each other. You can join one loop of each strip at a time (a 1x1 cable join, demonstrated here) or groups of two or more loops (2x2 cable join, and so on). The loops can be twisted or untwisted when they are joined to produce different effects.

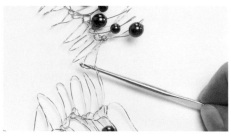

1 Lay the strips side by side. Insert the hook into the first loop of the first strip and then into the first loop of the second strip.

2 Pull the loop of the second strip through the loop of the first strip.

3 Insert the hook into the next loop of the first strip and pull this through the loop on the hook. Continue joining loops from alternate strips in this way.

4 When you reach the end, pull the tail from one of the strips through the last loop on the hook. Draw the loose end of the tail through the new loop on the hook to fasten off.

Cable heading

The edges of a hairpin strip can be embellished in a variety of ways. A cable heading involves slip-stitching the loops of the strip through each other. Guidelines of red yarn are used to help distinguish the front and back of the loops.

1 Insert the hook into the first loop and then into the second loop. Pull the second loop though the first loop.

2 Insert the hook into the next loop and pull this through the loop on the hook.

3 Continue in this way along the strip. When you reach the end, pull the tail from the strip through the last loop on the hook, then fasten off in the same was as for a cable join. Remove the guidelines if you have used any.

UNDERSTANDING patterns

The most important thing is to check that you start off with the correct number of stitches in the foundation row or ring, and then work through the instructions row by row or round by round exactly as stated. All of the patterns in this book use written instructions rather than charts.

Crochet abbreviations

The main abbreviations used in this book are:

bch—beaded chain
beg—begin(ning)
bpsc—back post single crochet
bsc—beaded single crochet
ch—chain
dc—double crochet
dc2tog—double crochet 2 together (1 stitch decreased)
fpsc—front post single crochet
hdc—half double crochet
hsc—hoop single crochet
lp(s)—loop(s)
pb—place bead
rev lp—reverse loop
RS—right side
sc—single crochet
sc2tog—single crochet 2 together (1 stitch decreased)
sl st—slip stitch
sp(s)—space(s)
st(s)—stitch(es)
tbl—through back loop
tr—treble or triple crochet
WS—wrong side
yo—yarn over

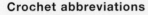

Essential information

Crochet patterns provide a list containing the size of the finished item, the materials and hook size required, the gauge of the piece (see box), and the abbreviations used in the instructions. Although many abbreviations are standardized, such as ch for chain and st for stitch, some of them vary, so always read the abbreviations before you start crocheting.

Repeats

When following pattern instructions, you will find that some of them appear within brackets and some are marked with an asterisk. Instructions that appear within brackets are to be repeated. For example, [1 dc in each of next 3 sts, ch 2] 4 times means that you work the three double crochet stitches and the two chains in the sequence stated four times in all. Asterisks (*) indicate the point to which you should return when you reach the phrase "repeat from *." They may also mark whole sets of instructions that are to be repeated. For example, "repeat from * to **" means repeat the instructions between the single and double asterisks.

You may also find asterisks used in instructions that tell you how to work any stitches remaining after the last complete repeat of a stitch sequence. For example, "repeat from *, ending with 1 sc in each of last 2 sts, turn," means that you have two stitches left at the end of the row after working the last repeat. In this case, work one single crochet into each of the last two stitches before turning to begin the next row.

Additional information

You may find a number enclosed in parentheses at the end of a row or round. This indicates the total number of stitches in that particular row or round. For example, (6 ch-4 sps) at the end of a round means that you have to work a chain-4 space six times in the round. Where there is information within parentheses, work that entire step in the indicated stitch.

Gauge

The term "gauge" refers to the number of stitches and rows contained in a given width and length of crochet fabric, usually 4" (10cm) square. Gauge varies from person to person, even when the same yarn and hook size are used. Most crochet patterns specify the required gauge, so if your gauge differs from the one given, the finished piece could be too big or too small. That is why it is usually important to check your gauge before starting a pattern. You can then adjust it if necessary by using a larger or smaller crochet hook from that specified in the pattern until you achieve the desired gauge. However, the jewelry projects in this book are made from such small pieces of crochet that a specific gauge is not required.

FINISHING **techniques**

A beautifully crocheted piece can easily be ruined by careless sewing up. Use a tapestry needle and a length of the yarn used to crochet the project, and select the method most suitable for the finished effect you want to achieve. Some crocheted pieces need to be blocked as well.

Fastening off

When your work is completed, you need to fasten off the yarn to stop it from raveling. This is called fastening off.

1 Cut the yarn, leaving a length of about 4–6" (10–15cm). Draw the loose end through the last loop on the hook.

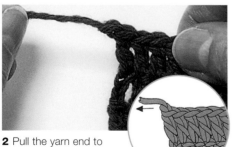

2 Pull the yarn end to tighten and secure it.

Weaving in ends

After fastening off the yarn, you need to weave all the loose ends into the work, running them through the stitches nearest to the yarn end. Thread the ends through a tapestry needle.

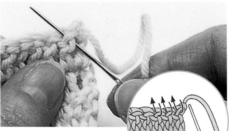

1 At the top edge of the work, weave the end through several stitches on the wrong side. Cut off the excess yarn.

2 At the lower edge of the work, weave the end through several stitches on the wrong side. Cut off the excess yarn.

Blocking

When all the ends are woven in, crochet fabrics usually need to be blocked to the correct size and shape. This is not really necessary with most of the projects in this book, although a few will benefit from this treatment.

Steam blocking

Pin the pieces right side downward onto a padded surface using glass-headed pins inserted at right angles to the edge of the crochet. Ease the crochet piece into shape. For natural fibers such as wool or cotton, set an iron on a steam setting. Hold the iron about 1" (2.5cm) above the fabric and allow the steam to penetrate for several seconds. Work in sections and avoid the iron touching the work. Allow to dry before removing the pins.

Cold-water blocking

Pin crochet pieces made from synthetic fibers as described above. Do not use an iron. When heat is applied to synthetics, they lose their luster and go very limp; in the worst cases you can melt the crochet and ruin your iron. When pinned out, spray the crochet fabric lightly with cold water until evenly moist but not soaked through. Allow to dry before taking out the pins.

Seams

There are several methods for joining pieces of crochet together. It is really a matter of personal preference unless a pattern specifies a method.

Backstitch seam

This creates a strong but non-elastic seam and is suitable for lightweight yarns. With right sides facing each other, pin together the pieces to be joined. Insert the pins at right angles to the edge evenly across the fabric. Thread a tapestry needle with yarn and work a straight row of backstitches along the edge.

Woven seam

Place the pieces to be joined side by side on a flat surface, with wrong sides facing up and edges together. Thread a tapestry needle with yarn. Working from right to left, place the needle under the loop of the first stitch on both pieces and draw the yarn through. Move along one stitch and repeat this process going from left to right. Continue to zigzag loosely from edge to edge. Pull the yarn tight every inch (2.5cm) or so, allowing the edges to join together. A woven seam gives a flatter, finer finish than a backstitch seam.

Single crochet seam

This creates a thick seam and looks neatest when the stitches are worked on the wrong side, so place the pieces to be joined right sides together unless you want to make a feature of the seam. Using a crochet hook and working from right to left, work a row of single crochet stitches through both layers.

Beaded single crochet seam

Thread the beads onto the yarn. Place the pieces to be joined wrong sides together. Using a crochet hook and working from right to left, work a row of beaded single crochet stitches through both layers. Intersperse the beaded single crochet stitches with plain stitches for a less heavily beaded result.

Overcast seam (whipstitch)

Pieces of crochet can be joined by overcasting the seam with whipstitch. The stitches can be worked through just the back of the crochet loops or the whole loops. Place the edges of the pieces to be joined together and thread a tapestry needle with yarn. Sew the seam with small, neat stitches

Slip-stitch seam

Place the pieces to be joined wrong sides together. Using a crochet hook and working from right to left, work a row of slip stitches through both layers. A slip-stitch seam creates an attractive ridge on the right side of the fabric.

FASTENINGS **and findings**

There is a huge selection of fastenings and findings now available, and the basic techniques used for attaching them can easily be adapted for different styles.

Attaching a clasp using crimps

Clasps can be threaded onto beading wire or strong synthetic beading thread and secured in place using crimps.

1 Cut a length of beading wire using wire cutters, allowing 1¼–1½" (3–4cm) extra at each end to attach the clasp. Thread on your beads as instructed in the pattern. Thread a crimp onto one end of the beading wire, then thread the wire through one end of the clasp.

A single crimp is sufficient if the beads are light, but use two crimps if the beads are heavy.

2 Thread the beading wire back through the crimp, leaving a loop that allows movement but looks neat.

3 Flatten the crimp with flat-nose pliers or use special crimping pliers if you have them. Slide the beads up to meet the crimp, passing them over the loose end of the thread if possible; if not, cut the loose end very close to the crimp and then slide back the beads. Add another crimp to the other end of the wire and attach the other end of the fastener in the same way, allowing for some movement but without the thread showing too much.

Sewing a clasp in place

Using doubled thread will make it easier to attach the clasp and create a stronger, more durable attachment.

1 Pass both ends of a length of beading thread through the eye of the needle.

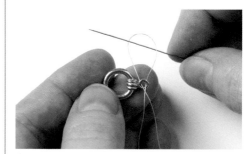

2 Take the needle through the fixing point on the clasp, leaving a loop of thread on the other side. Secure the thread by passing the needle through the loop.

3 Pull the doubled thread firmly to secure it to the ring. Rethread the needle and sew firmly in place.

Beaded loop fastener

Thread on enough beads to make a loop large enough to slip over the button or bead. Pass the needle back down through the first few beads and into the main body of the work. Knot securely, then take the needle back up through the loop of beads two or three more times for added security, knotting each time.

Opening and closing jump rings

Open a jump ring by twisting it apart using two pairs of pliers. Do not pull the ring apart because this will strain the wire; instead, twist one pair of pliers toward you, and the other away from you. Slip the ring through the crochet piece or finding as required, then twist the ring closed.

Making wire loops

Use pliers to form simple loops in head pins and eye pins so that you can attach them to crochet pieces and findings such as ear wires.

1 Use wire cutters to trim the wire if necessary. Position round-nose pliers about ¼" (5mm) from the end of the wire and use them to bend the wire toward you to about 45 degrees.

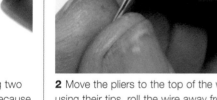

2 Move the pliers to the top of the wire and, using their tips, roll the wire away from you to form a small, neat loop. Leave the loop slightly open to allow another component to be attached; squeeze it shut with pliers afterward.

Attaching earring findings

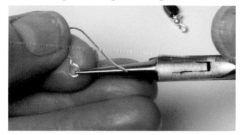

Using the loop

Sew in place by stitching through the loop, or open the loop so that you can slip it through the crochet piece or another finding. Hold the finding in one hand and use pliers to twist open the loop sideways a little, in the same way as a jump ring. Twist it closed when attached.

Sewing around an ear post

Make a small back stitch on the reverse of the earring. Stitch across the back of the finding and back to the start point several times. Repeat this at a point 90 degrees to the first set of stitches.

Attaching pin backs

Thread a needle and make a small backstitch on the reverse of the pin. Stitch through each fixing point on the pin back several times.

Finishing threads and wires

Finish off beading thread and wire securely by weaving the ends back and forth through several stitches or beads, tying a knot occasionally. Add a drop of seam sealant to the ends of threads for extra security if desired, then trim close to the work. Always smooth the ends of wires tightly into the work so that there are no sharp points.

CHAPTER 2

Necklaces

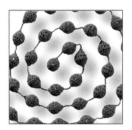

What better way to set off an outfit than with a beautiful crochet necklace. Choose from playful designs, such as the big bead necklace and circle necklace—both of which can also be worn as belts—or opt for something elegant and sophisticated, such as the surface crochet choker and hairpin bead necklace.

BIG **bead necklace**

Skill level
Easy

This necklace is the perfect choice if you like long or multilayer necklaces, and you can even wear it around your waist as a belt. You can achieve a different look by choosing yarns of different textures. The thin synthetic thread used here produces a sleek look that you can wear year-round with anything from jeans to an evening dress.

MAKING THE NECKLACE

Crochet around the first bead as follows.

Foundation ring: Ch 4 and join with sl st to form a ring.

Round 1: Ch 1, 8 sc in ring, join with sl st in first sc.

Round 2: Ch 3 (count as 1 dc), 1 dc in same st as join, 2 dc in each sc across, join with sl st in top of beg ch-3 (16 dc).

Round 3: Ch 3, 1 dc in next dc, *2 dc in next dc, 1 dc in each of next 2 dc; repeat from * around to last 2 sts, 2 dc in next dc, 1 dc in last dc, join with sl st in top of beg ch-3 (21 dc).

Round 4: Ch 3, 1 dc in each dc around, join with sl st in top of beg ch-3 (21 dc). Insert bead.

Round 5: Ch 3, 1 dc in next dc, *dc2tog, 1 dc in each of next 2 dc; repeat from * around to last 3 sts, dc2tog, 1 dc in last dc, join with sl st in top of beg ch-3 (16 dc).

Round 6: Ch 1, *sc2tog; repeat from * around, join with sl st in first sc (8 sc).

Round 7: Repeat round 6 (4 sc). Bead complete. Ch 10, join with sl st in fourth ch from hook. Repeat from round 1 until desired length of necklace is reached.

After the last bead is complete, work a fastening loop as follows: Ch 35, sl st in 25th ch from hook to form fastening loop, ch 1, work 30 sc in loop, 1 sc in each ch to bead, join with sl st in first sc of round 7.

Fasten off.

FINISHING

With a tapestry needle, weave in all ends.

Tools and materials

- Hook: steel, size 8 (1.5mm)
- Thread: laceweight nylon crochet thread in the color of your choice; to calculate quantity, measure out several yards or meters of thread, work pattern to end of first bead, subtract length not used, then multiply length used by number of beads plus 1 bead (to allow for fastening)
- Beads: 20mm glass beads; quantity depends on desired length of necklace (35 beads are used here)
- Notions: tapestry needle

Finished size

Adjustable; sample = 56" (142cm) long

Abbreviations

beg—begin(ning)
ch—chain
dc—double crochet
dc2tog—double crochet 2 together (1 stitch decreased)
sc—single crochet
sc2tog—single crochet 2 together (1 stitch decreased)
sl st—slip stitch
st(s)—stitch(es)

REMINDER: CROCHETING AROUND BEADS

1 Work a foundation chain of the required length and join with a slip stitch to form a ring.

2 Work the first round into the foundation ring. The first round here is worked in single crochet, but other stitches can be used instead.

3 Work the next round (here, double crochet), increasing stitches by working two stitches into each stitch of the previous round as instructed.

4 Work two more rounds, increasing as instructed. Adjust the number of rounds if using different-size beads from those specified.

5 Insert the bead. Gradually decrease the number of stitches on subsequent rounds by working two stitches together, until the bead is covered completely.

BARREL **bead necklace**

This necklace is made using a fluffy mohair yarn that has a metallic thread running through it. If you cannot find this type of yarn, purchase a separate metallic thread to use in conjunction with a plain mohair or other type of novelty yarn. Never be afraid to adapt and experiment so that you get a piece of jewelry you really like.

MAKING THE NECKLACE

BARREL BEAD (make 5)

Foundation ring: Ch 5 and join with sl st to form a ring.

Round 1: Ch 1, 1 sc in each ch around. Continue working in rounds, 1 sc in back loop of each sc, until barrel measures 1¼" (3cm) long. Fasten off and use a tapestry needle to weave in all ends. Slide each barrel onto a chopstick or similar-size knitting needle while you make the next one. This will help the bead retain its shape. Randomly sew 30 size 8° seed beads onto one of the barrel beads; use this as the center bead.

CENTER CORD

If using a metallic mohair yarn, as here, separate the metallic thread from the rest of the yarn and make the center cord using the metallic thread only. If not using yarn that will separate easily, use it whole or select a coordinating metallic-type thread instead.

Make a chain about 18" (46cm) long. Work 1 sc in second ch from hook and in each ch across. Fasten off.

Thread center cord through the barrel beads, tying a loose knot between each of the beads to separate them. Leave about 2½" (6cm) of cord at each end.

CORD EXTENSION

Join the yarn (do not separate it any more) to right-hand end of center cord and chain about 5" (13cm); ch 6 more for making a fastening loop.

Next row: Sl st in seventh ch from hook and in each ch of extension, 1 sc in end of center cord. Fasten off.

Join yarn to other end of center cord and work as for first side, omitting the extra ch 6 and working first sl st in second ch from hook.

Tie a knot in each end of center cord, previously left unknotted.

Sew a size 8° seed bead into each stitch—or about ¼" (6mm) apart—along each end of the cord extension. Sew a button to the left-hand end of the cord extension, with three size 8° seed beads between the holes on the button.

With a tapestry needle, weave in all ends.

TASSEL

Using a beading needle, attach beading thread to the middle of the center barrel bead using several small stitches. Using size 11° seed beads, thread on 5 seeds, the focal bead, 1 seed, 1 bugle, 1 seed, 1 accent bead, 2 seeds, 1 bugle, 2 seeds, 1 accent bead, 2 seeds, 1 bugle, and 5 seeds. Skipping the last 3 seed beads, thread the needle back up through the remaining beads and make a couple of small stitches in the barrel bead in same place as you started.

Repeat this procedure four more times, taking each tassel drop through the focal bead. When the final tassel drop has been completed, make several small stitches in the barrel bead to secure. Fasten off.

FINISHING

Lay necklace lengthwise on a towel, making sure the beaded chain extension is not twisted. To block, pin necklace down on towel and spray lightly with water. Allow to dry.

Tools and materials

- Hook: size G–6 (4mm)
- Yarn: 45yds (41m) worsted-weight mohair or other type of novelty yarn containing some metallic thread; a purple/orange mix mohair is used here, but choose a color that tones well with the beads you select
- Beads: 70 size 8° seed beads and 90 size 11° seed beads in pink/purple/pearlescent tones; 16 orange 7mm bugle beads; 10 purple 5mm flower accent beads; 1 pink/purple 10mm round focal bead
- Notions: tapestry needle; chopstick or knitting needle; ⅝" (15mm) gold button; beading needle; beading thread to match bead colors

Finished size

20" (51cm) long

Abbreviations

ch—chain
sc—single crochet
sl st—slip stitch

See also
Tubular crochet, page 31
Sewing on beads and sequins, page 107

Only basic stitches are required to work this stylish choker, so this project is ideal for beginners. The pattern includes instructions for two sizes, so you can be sure of a comfortable fit.

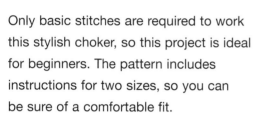

HOOP **choker**

MAKING THE CHOKER

These directions are written for the small size, with changes for the large size in brackets. When there is only one number, work for both sizes. Using a beading needle, string beads onto thread.

Row 1: Starting with a slipknot on the hook, work 151 [163] sc loosely onto neck ring (work sc sts right around the metal ring), turn.

Row 2: Ch 1, 1 sc in first st, *skip 2 sts, 5 dc in next st, skip 2 sts, 1 sc in next st; repeat from * across, turn.

Row 3: Ch 3 (counts as 1 dc), 2 dc in first st, *skip 2 sts, 1 sc in next st, skip 2 sts, 5 dc in next st, repeat from * across, ending with 3 dc in last st, turn.

Row 4: Ch 1, 1 bsc in each st across. Fasten off.

FINISHING

With a tapestry needle, weave in all ends.

Skill level
Easy

Tools and materials
- Hook: size B–1 (2.25mm)
- Thread: 25yds (23m) aqua rayon embroidery thread
- Beads: 151 [163] blue size 6º seed beads
- Findings: 16 [18]" (41 [46] cm) circumference sterling silver neck ring
- Notions: beading needle; tapestry needle

Finished size
16 [18]" (40 [46] cm) circumference

See also
Crocheting around hoops or rings, page 37
Beaded crochet, page 38

Abbreviations
bsc—beaded single crochet sc—single crochet
ch—chain st(s)—stitch(es)
dc—double crochet

MAKING THE KEEPER

Using a beading needle, string beads onto thread in the following order: 1 glasses keeper, *A, B, A, C, D, C, A, B; repeat from *, ending with one more A bead and second glasses keeper.

Starting keeper: Make slipknot in thread and put loop onto crochet hook. Bring silver loop of keeper close to knot and ch 1, insert hook into silver loop of keeper and work 1 sc.

Working chain: *Ch 2, 1 bch; repeat from * across.

Finishing keeper: End with ch 1 to attach second keeper and work 1 sc in silver loop of keeper to secure it solidly.
Fasten off.

FINISHING

With a tapestry needle, weave in all ends.

Glasses KEEPER

This very simple glasses keeper is an ideal project for beginners. Avoid large chunky beads because the added weight will make the glasses seem heavy on the ears and bridge of the nose. It is easy to change the color scheme to match the frames of your glasses, or you could make several in different colors to coordinate with whatever you are wearing.

Tools and materials

- Hook: size B–1 (2.25mm)
- String: 18yds (17m) size 6 no-stretch nylon beading thread
- Beads: 31 silver-plated 5mm round beads (A); 20 black onyx 6mm round beads (B), 20 zebra-striped size 6º round glass seed beads (C); 10 hematite 8mm faceted round beads (D)
- Findings: 2 silver-plated glasses keepers with black elastic
- Notions: beading needle; tapestry needle

Skill level
Easy

Finished size
26" (66cm) long

Abbreviations
bch—beaded chain
ch—chain
sc—single crochet

See also
Beaded crochet, page 38

CIRCLE **necklace**

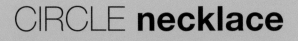

Skill level
Easy; if this is your first project, try a
few rings without beads for practice

This funky Sixties-style necklace
can also be worn as a hipster belt;
simply adjust the number of circles if
you need to. You could easily make
matching earrings by attaching a
crocheted circle to an earring finding
by a length of chain; try dangling
several circles of different sizes from
chains of different lengths.

MAKING THE NECKLACE

Using a sewing or beading needle, thread all the beads onto the yarn. Starting with a slipknot on the hook, work all sc and beo cts right around each plastic ring.

Circle 1: Ch 1, 3 sc, 1 bsc, [5 sc, 1 bsc] 3 times, 2 sc, ch 5 (half of ring is covered).

Circles 2–20: 3 sc, 1 bsc, [5 sc, 1 bsc] 3 times, 2 sc, ch 5.

Circle 21: 3 sc, 1 bsc, [5 sc, 1 bsc] 3 times, 2 sc, ch 20, sl st in 14th ch from hook to form a fastening loop, 19 sc around fastening loop (to reinforce it), join with sl st in first sc of fastening loop, ch 5, join with sl st in last sc of circle 21. Continuing over other half of ring, work *3 sc, 1 bsc, [5 sc, 1 bsc] 3 times, 2 sc, join with sl st in first sc of circle, ch 5, join with sl st in last sc* of previous circle.

Circles 20–2: Repeat from * to * of circle 21.

Circle 1: 3 sc, 1 bsc, [5 sc, 1 bsc] 3 times, 2 sc, join with sl st in first sc, ch 9, join with sl st in first sc.
Fasten off.

BUTTON

Foundation ring: Ch 4 and join with sl st to form a ring.

Round 1: Ch 1, 8 bsc in ring, join with sl st in first bsc.

Round 2: Ch 1, 2 bsc in each bsc, join with sl st in first bsc (12 sc).

Round 3: Ch 1, 1 bsc in each bsc, join with sl st in first bsc.

Round 4: Ch 1, [bsc2tog] 6 times, join with sl st in first bsc (6 bsc).
Stuff some tightly rolled yarn into the ball.

Round 5: Ch 1, [bsc2tog] 3 times, join with sl st in first bsc (3 bsc).
Fasten off.

FINISHING

With a tapestry needle, weave in all ends. Sew the button onto the middle of the ch-9 loop at the end of circle 1.

Tools and materials

- Hook: steel, size 4 (2mm)
- Yarn: fine gold Lurex; to calculate quantity, measure out several yards or meters of yarn, work pattern to end of circle 1 (halfway around plastic ring), then double length used and multiply this figure by number of circles plus 1 circle (to allow for fastening)
- Beads: 207 silver 2mm cylinder beads (adjust quantity if a different number of circles are worked)
- Notions: sewing or beading needle; 21 plastic 1⅛" (30mm) diameter rings (adjust quantity as required); tapestry needle

Finished size
36" (91cm) long

Abbreviations
bsc—beaded single crochet
bsc2tog—work 2 beaded single crochet together (1 stitch decreased)
ch—chain
sc—single crochet
sl st—slip stitch
st(s)—stitch(es)
[ ]—work step in brackets number of times indicated

See also
Crocheting around hoops or rings, page 37
Beaded crochet, page 38

REMINDER: BEADED SINGLE CROCHET AROUND A RING AND BEADED DECREASING

 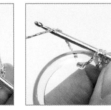  

1 To work bsc around a ring, insert the hook through the ring, wrap the yarn over the hook, and draw the yarn through the ring toward you.

2 Push a bead up the yarn to sit at the center of the ring. Wrap the yarn over the hook again, this time outside of the ring.

3 Pull the yarn through both loops on the hook to complete the stitch. Make sure the bead is at the center of the ring.

4 To work bsc2tog, insert the hook into the first stitch, yarn over, pull yarn through stitch, then push a bead up the yarn to sit just under the hook.

5 Insert the hook in the next stitch, yarn over, pull yarn through stitch, yarn over, then finish by pulling yarn through all three loops on the hook.

The front of this sumptuously beaded purse is embellished with crocheted flowers, and the purse is finished with a fringe and a strap of strung beads. The back is worked in unbeaded single crochet so that the purse remains quite flexible and is comfortable to wear.

AMULET **purse**

Skill level
Intermediate

Tools and materials

- Hook: size D–3 (3.25mm)
- Thread/wire: 25yds (23m) silver rayon thread, pearl cotton, or similar; 5yds (4.5m) 32-gauge (0.2mm) silver wire
- Beads: 1oz (28g) size 8° and size 11° seed bead mix; 28 medium-size accent beads; 2 leaf-shaped glass beads
- Notions: tapestry needle; beading needle; strong beading thread; seam sealant; sewing thread to match overall color scheme

Finished size

Purse = 2½" high x 1¾" wide (6.5 x 4.5cm) excluding fringe
Strap = 26" (66cm) long

Abbreviations

bsc—beaded single crochet
ch—chain
dc—double crochet
sc—single crochet
sl st—slip stitch
st(s)—stitch(es)
WS—wrong side

See also

Beaded crochet, page 38
Wire crochet, page 39
Adding a fringe, page 83
Sewing on beads and sequins, page 107

MAKING THE PURSE

Thread about 60" (1.5m) of seed beads randomly onto rayon thread and work the front of the purse as follows.

Foundation chain: Ch 13.
Row 1: 1 sc in second ch from hook, 1 bsc in each of next 10 sts using 2 or 3 beads at random for each bsc, 1 sc in last st, turn (12 sts).
Row 2: Ch 1, 1 sc in each st to end, turn.
Row 3: Ch 1, 1 sc in next st, 1 bsc in each of next 10 sts using 1, 2, or 3 beads at random for each bsc, 1 sc in last st, turn.
Repeat rows 2–3 until front measures 2½" (6.5cm). Work the back of the purse in sc (without beads) until it measures the same as front. Fasten off.

JOINING PURSE SEAMS

Fold purse in half, WS together. With back facing you, join thread with sl st through both thicknesses at the top left-hand corner.
Working through both thicknesses, work a row of bsc down left-hand side, across base, and up right-hand side.
Work a row of bsc (use 3–5 beads at random) across the top of front section only. Fasten off.
With a tapestry needle, weave in all ends.

STRAP

Using a beading needle and with front of purse facing you, join beading thread to top right-hand corner of purse by running the thread through some of the beads near the corner, knotting it every now and then to secure. Add a drop of seam sealant to each knot for extra security. Thread on seed beads and accent beads in the arrangement of your choice (save nine accent beads for the fringe). When you reach halfway—about 13" (33cm)—add a distinctive accent bead if you would like to separate the two halves of the strap. Continue threading beads, this time in the reverse order to create a symmetrical strap design. Attach strap to top left-hand corner of purse, securing the thread as before.

FRINGE

With the front of the purse facing you, find the center of the base and attach beading thread securely. Thread on 7 size 8°, 7 size 11°, 1 accent, 3 size 11°, 1 size 8°, and 5 size 11° beads. Skipping the last 3 beads, thread the needle back up through the remaining beads, taking care not to split the thread inside them. Secure thread at the top of this first fringe with one or two knots, then move across to the next fringe position. Take thread through fabric a couple of times at each fringe position for extra security. Working outward to one side of the purse, make four more fringes of decreasing lengths using the bead arrangement of your choice. Repeat for the other side to create symmetrical fringing, then secure the thread as before.

FLOWERS (make 3)

Foundation ring: Using wire and sewing thread held together, ch 4 and join with sl st to form a ring.
Round 1: Ch 3, 11 dc in ring.
Fasten off.

FINISHING

With the front of the purse facing you, sew the flowers to the top left-hand corner. Sew one size 8° seed bead topped with one size 11° seed bead to each flower center. Around one flower edge, stitch one size 11° bead at the top of each dc. Repeat for remaining two flowers if desired. Sew leaf beads to the purse at the base of the flowers to create a pleasing arrangement.

This necklace is perfect for displaying pretty accent beads, which are framed on a bed of seed beads in complementary colors. It is a good idea to place the wire in a small drawstring bag to help keep it under control when making this project. You will find a pair of matching earrings on page 102.

SURFACE **crochet choker**

Skill level
Intermediate

Tools and materials
- Hook: size B–1 (2.25mm)
- Wire: 24yd (22m) roll of 32-gauge (0.2mm) colored wire
- Beads: 1oz (28g) size 11° seed bead mix; 1oz (28g) size 8° seed bead mix; 16 bicone or round accent beads; 2 extra round accent beads
- Notions: small drawstring bag (optional); beading needle; strong beading thread; seam sealant; ⅝" (15mm) shank button

Finished size
19½" (49.5cm) long

Abbreviations
bch—beaded chain
bsc—beaded single crochet
ch—chain
RS—right side
sc—single crochet
sl st—slip stitch
st(s)—stitch(es)
WS—wrong side

See also
Surface crochet, page 36
Beaded crochet, page 38
Wire crochet, page 39

MAKING THE CHOKER

Randomly thread about 75" (190cm) of size 11° seed beads onto the wire.

Foundation chain: Work bch for 17½" (44.5cm) using 3 beads for each bch. Do not turn.

Row 1: Sl st back along chain, bringing up 3 beads for each sl st.
Fasten off.

Twist the wire ends together a few times to secure; using a beading needle, take the wire ends down through as many beads as possible to hide and secure them.

Lay work on a flat surface and gently press flat, making sure the chain is not twisted.

Find the center of the chain. Mark 4" (10cm) on each side of center with a thread.

With WS facing, rejoin beaded wire to top loop of the marked right-hand side.

Row 2 (WS): Ch 1, 1 bsc in each st between markers using 3 beads for each st. Give each st a gentle tug and squeeze before working the next st (this will help the work to lay flat). Turn.

Row 3: Ch 1, 1 sc (without beads) in each st between markers, turn.

Row 4: Repeat row 2.
Fasten off.

Leaving the seed beads already on the wire to use later, randomly add about 18" (45.5cm) of mixed accent beads and seed beads in both sizes onto wire, spacing the accent beads so that they do not follow each other too closely.

With WS facing, join wire to necklace about 1" (2.5cm) before right-hand marker.

Row 5: Bringing up a bead or two for each sl st, work a row of beaded surface crochet along the chain section, then along the "ditch" made by the previously worked row of sc and along the other end of the chain section, about 1" (2.5cm) after marker. Fasten off.

Note: You can bring up 2 or 3 seed beads at a time if you like, but depending on the size of your accent beads, you may prefer to use only one of those at a time.

Row 6: With WS facing, join wire just under the right-hand marker and work one more row of beaded surface crochet on this lower edge of the center section, finishing just under the left-hand marker. Fasten off and hide wire as before.

FASTENING LOOP
With RS facing, attach beading thread to right end of necklace, knotting it around wire several times to secure (add a drop of seam sealant if desired). Thread on 1 size 8° bead, 1 accent bead, and enough size 11° beads to make a loop big enough to fit your button (sample uses 20 beads). Take thread back down through both the accent and size 8° beads, then weave the thread through the beads along the chain section for about 2" (5cm), knotting thread around the wire and adding a drop of seam sealant for extra security. Finally, go back up through the beads on the chain section and through the fastening loop, then back down into beads on the chain section again, tying another knot or two around the wire for extra security. Fasten off by cutting thread as close to the final bead as you can.

BUTTON CLOSURE
Join thread to other end of necklace as before. Thread on 1 size 8° bead, 1 accent bead, 1 size 8° bead, then the button, taking thread back around the shank several times. Add 1 more size 8° bead and take thread back down through shank and beads and secure as for other side.

FINISHING
Weave any wire ends through as many beads as you can and cut off close to the final bead. Gently manipulate the necklace with your fingers to make sure it lays flat.

Changing stitch heights creates the shells on this necklace. The classic monochrome color scheme featured here is perfect for evening wear, but you could use any colors you like. Try making the band in one color, then changing to another color to work the shells.

SHELL **necklace**

MAKING THE NECKLACE

Foundation chain: Ch 113.
Row 1: 1 sc in second ch from hook and in each ch across, turn (112 sc).
Row 2: Ch 1, 1 sc in each sc to end, turn.
Row 3: Ch 1, *1 sc in each of next 4 sts, ch 2, 1 bch, ch 2, 1 sc in same st as last sc (bead picot made); repeat from * 9 times (10 bead picots total).
Work shells: [1 sc in each of next 8 sc, turn, ch 7, sl st in eighth sc from hook before ch-7 (15th st from hook), turn. Into ch-7 sp, work (1 sc, 2 hdc, 3 dc, 2 tr, 2 dc, 2 hdc, 1 sc)] 4 times.
Continue as follows: 1 sc in next sc, ch 2, 1 bch, ch 2, 1 sc in same st as last

sc; repeat from * 9 times (10 bead picots total), 1 sc in each st to end.
Fasten off.
With necklace facing you, join yarn to bottom right-hand end, then ch 7 and join with sl st to top edge to make a fastening loop.

FINISHING
With a tapestry needle, weave in all ends. Sew a button to the left-hand end of necklace. To block, pin necklace down on a towel and spray lightly with water. Allow to dry.

Skill level
Intermediate

Tools and materials
• Hook: size B–1 (2.25mm)
• Thread: 80yds (73m) black size 4 crochet cotton
• Beads: 68 white and/or clear size 8° seed beads
• Notions: tapestry needle; ⅝" (15mm) button

Finished size
20½" (52cm) long

See also
Beaded crochet, page 38

Abbreviations

bch—beaded chain	st(s)—stitch(es)
ch—chain	tr—treble crochet
dc—double crochet	[ ]—work step in brackets
hdc—half double crochet	number of times indicated
sc—single crochet	( )—work step in parentheses
sl st—slip stitch	in indicated stitch
sp—space	

MAKING THE NECKLACE

Crochet around each bead in the yarn of your choice as follows.

Foundation ring: Ch 4 and join with sl st to form a ring.

Round 1: Ch 1, 8 sc in ring, join with sl st in first sc (8 sc).

Round 2: Ch 1, 2 sc in same st as join and in each sc around, join with sl st in first sc (16 sc).

Round 3: Ch 1, 1 sc in same st as join and in next sc, *2 sc in next sc, 1 sc in each of next 2 sc; repeat from * around to last 2 sts, 2 sc in next sc, 1 sc in last sc, join with sl st in first sc (21 sc).

Rounds 4–5: Ch 1, 1 sc in same st as join and in each sc around, join with sl st in first sc (21 sc). Insert bead.

Round 6: Ch 1, 1 sc in same st as join and in next sc, *sc2tog, 1 sc in each of next 2 sc; repeat from * around to last 3 sts, sc2tog, 1 sc in last sc, join with sl st in first sc (16 sc).

Round 7: Ch 1, *sc2tog; repeat from * around, join with sl st in first sc (8 sc).

Round 8: Repeat round 7 (4 sc). Bead complete. Fasten off and use hook to push ends of thread inside to hide them. Make the cord by working a chain of the desired length using mohair or ribbon yarn.

Tools and materials
- Hook: steel, size 8 (1.5mm)
- Thread/yarn: scraps of laceweight nylon crochet thread in different colors; mohair or ribbon yarn for cord; novelty yarn for attaching beads
- Beads: 20mm glass beads; quantity depends on desired length of necklace (14 beads are used here)
- Notions: tapestry needle

Multicolor NECKLACE

Skill level
Easy

FINISHING

Mark center 15" (38cm) of cord for bead placement. Using a tapestry needle, thread a length of novelty yarn through top of crocheted part of a bead, catching several stitches and leaving a tail. Run through a chain stitch on cord in desired area between markers, wrap around cord several times, then tie to tail. Repeat with remaining beads. If novelty yarn is thin or weak, or if beads are heavy, use a double strand to attach. Tie the cord with a bow for closure.

This necklace provides the perfect opportunity for combining lots of colors. You could also use a variety of different yarns. For example, use nylon yarn to crochet around some beads, and mohair to crochet around others.

Finished size
Adjustable; sample = 39" (99cm) long from end to end and 15" (38cm) in bead area

Abbreviations
ch—chain
sc—single crochet
sc2tog—single crochet 2 together (1 stitch decreased)
sl st—slip stitch
st(s)—stitch(es)

See also
Crocheting around beads, page 51

GEMSTONE **lariat**

Skill level
Lariat = easy
Motifs = intermediate

This lariat necklace looks lovely with or without the motifs. The motifs can be fastened to the necklace permanently, or you can make a loop at the top of each shape so that you can add or remove them whenever you like. You could easily adapt this design to make a hipster belt, or use the motifs as pendants.

MAKING THE LARIAT

String beads onto A in a random order, mixing them up as much as possible.

Using larger hook, work 1 sc right around the jasper ring.

Work the lariat in bch until total length is 26" (66cm) or as long as you want it to be. Bring up 1 bead for each bch or 2 beads if they are very small. For an oval bead, you might have to work 2 or 3 ch to create a little cage, bring up the bead, and work 1 more ch to fasten it.

Fasten off.

SUN MOTIF

Round 1: Using larger hook and A, ch 4, 9 dc in fourth ch from hook, then join with sl st in top of beg ch (10 dc counting beg ch-3 as 1 dc).

Round 2: Ch 5 (counts as 1 dc, ch 2), 1 dc in same st as join, ch 2, ([1 dc, ch 2] twice) in each st around, join with sl st in third ch of beg ch-5 (20 dc).

Ch 5 or 6 and fasten to lariat with sl st, or ch 15 and form a loop by joining with sl st to first ch.

Fasten off.

MOON MOTIF

Note: For moon and star motifs, work with B using larger hook or change to smaller steel hook if your stitches are too loose.

Row 1: Ch 13, sl st in second ch from hook, 1 sc in each of next 2 ch, 2 hdc in each of next 2 ch, 2 dc in each of next 2 ch, 2 hdc in each of next 2 ch, 1 sc in each of next 2 ch, sl st in last ch, turn.

Row 2: Do not chain, sl st in first sc, 1 sc in each of next 2 sts, 1 hdc in each of next 10 sts, 1 sc in each of next 2 sts, sl st in last sc and in next sl st.

Fasten to lariat or work loop as for sun motif.

STAR MOTIF

Round 1: Ch 4, 14 dc in fourth ch from hook, then join with sl st in top of beg ch (15 dc counting beg ch-3 as 1 dc).

Round 2: *Ch 9, sl st in fourth ch from hook, 1 sc in next ch, 1 hdc in each of next 2 ch, 1 dc in each of next 2 ch; skip next 2 sts on circle, sl st in following st; repeat from * 4 more times, ending with sl st at end of round.

Fasten to lariat or work loop as for sun motif.

FINISHING

With a tapestry needle, weave in all ends.

Tools and materials
- Hook: size B–1 (2.25mm); steel, size 8 (1.5mm) or 9 (1.4mm)
- Thread: 11yds (10m) size 12 metallic tapestry braid (A); small amount of size 10 embroidery thread (B)
- Beads: 3½oz (100g) green beads in assorted shapes, sizes, and shades
- Notions: ¾" (20mm) diameter green jasper ring; tapestry needle

Finished size
26" (66cm) long

Abbreviations
bch—beaded chain
beg—begin(ning)
ch—chain
dc—double crochet
hdc—half double crochet
sc—single crochet
sl st—slip stitch
st(s)—stitch(es)
[ ]—work step in brackets number of times indicated
( )—work step in parentheses in indicated stitch

See also
Crocheting around hoops or rings, page 37
Beaded crochet, page 38

This necklace incorporates two designs of crocheted beads, both made using wire and hairpin crochet. You can make this necklace from different source beads than those featured here, as well as vary the stringing arrangement and overall length; use the materials list as a guideline for quantities and sizes.

HAIRPIN **bead necklace**

Skill level
Advanced

Tools and materials

- Hook: steel, size 7 (1.65mm)
- Hairpin loom
- Wire: 12yds (11m) 28-gauge (0.3mm) gold wire
- Beads: 78 red 5mm chip garnet beads (A); 7 red 6mm round garnet beads (B); 109 gold 2mm seed beads (C); 16 opalescent gold size 8° seed beads (D); 1 metallic 11mm oval glass bead (E); 1 gold 6mm round metal bead (F); 800 amber size 11° hex cylinder seed beads (G)
- Findings: 2 gold crimps; 1½yds (1.4m) beading wire; 1 gold clasp and jump ring
- Notions: flat-nose pliers (optional)

Finished size

Flower bead = 1¼" (3cm) diameter
Bicone bead = ¾" (2cm) stringing length
Total length = 50" (127cm)

Abbreviations

RS—right side
WS—wrong side
[ ]—work step in brackets number of times indicated

See also

Hairpin crochet, pages 40–41
Fastenings and findings, pages 46–47

MAKING THE NECKLACE

FLOWER BEAD (make 3)
Thread the beads onto the gold wire in the following order: C, [A, A, C] 12 times.

Work strip: Set the loom to ½" (13mm) and use a twisted loop on the starting pin instead of a slipknot, taking care that the first bead is caught in this first loop. Catch a C bead in every other loop made on the hairpin loom; they will line up along one side of the loom. Catch an A bead in every stitch of the hairpin strip. Work 25 loops in total, then fasten off. Leave 3" (7.5cm) tails at beginning and end.

Make circle: Loops on one side of the strip will be bare for the inside of the rosette; loops on the other side of the strip will contain C beads for the outside "petals" of the rosette. Cut 6" (15cm) of wire and thread it through the empty loops; the RS will have A beads situated closer to the loops with no beads. Twist ends of wire tightly on WS, causing the strip to curl upon itself into a circle. The circle should lay with the beginning and ending sides of the strip next to each other, and with the inner loops of the strip forming a slight dome. Use the tails of the strip to weave the beginning and end of the strip together so that the strip now forms a continuous circle. Secure and trim all the wire ends.

Make petals: While holding the beads in the outer loops, twist the wire with fingers or flat-nose pliers, being careful not to overtwist and break the wire.

BICONE BEAD (make 3)
Thread 10 A beads onto the gold wire.
Work strip: Set loom to ¾" (2cm) and use a twisted loop on the starting pin instead of a slipknot.

Catch an A bead in every other stitch of the hairpin strip; they will align on one side (RS) of the strip only. Work 20 loops in total, then fasten off. Leave 4" (10cm) tails at beginning and end.

Make circle: Use the tails of the strip to weave the beginning and end of the strip together so that the strip now forms a cylinder, keeping the RS facing outward. Run each tail through the empty loops at each side and tighten to close the loops into a cone at each side. Secure and trim all the wire ends.

STRINGING THE NECKLACE
Refer to bead patterns box below when stringing the necklace, but feel free to vary the design according to the beads you have and the look you would like to achieve.

Start with clasp: Thread a crimp and then about 12 G beads onto the beading wire. String clasp over G beads, bring end of wire back through crimp, and tighten the crimp so that the beads form a nice loop holding the clasp. Add a C bead.

Stringing the beads: Space each of the following bead groups with a G group—[D group] twice, [B group, D group] twice, D group, bicone group, B group, [D group] twice, flower group, metallic group, D group, B group, flower group, bicone group, D group, flower group, B group, [D group] twice, bicone group, B group, [D group] twice, oval group, D group, B group, [D group] twice.

End with clasp: Thread on a G group, a C bead, then a crimp. Add about 10 more G beads and the jump ring. Thread the wire end back through the crimp and tighten so that the beads form a nice loop holding the jump ring. Trim the wire end.

BEAD PATTERNS

G group—Vary the number of G beads in each group, making some smaller and some larger, but keeping the number to about 10.

D group—String beads in this order: C, D, C.

B group—String beads in this order: C, B, C.

Bicone group—String bicone beads through the closing loops at each end in this order: C, bicone bead, C.

Flower group—String flower beads through the openings of the spine in the strip (between the A beads), running in on one side, across the back, and out through the opposite side. String beads in this order: C, one end of flower bead from front to back, C, number of G beads required to span back of flower bead, C, through flower bead from back to front, C.

Metallic group—String beads in this order: C, F, C.

Oval group—String beads in this order: C, D, E, D, C.

CHAPTER 3

Bracelets

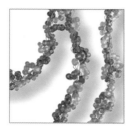

From delicate beaded bangles to funky felted bracelets, there is something in this chapter to suit everyone's taste. Three watch straps are also included, which can easily be adapted into standard bracelets if you prefer, and the beaded chain bracelet can also be worn as a necklace.

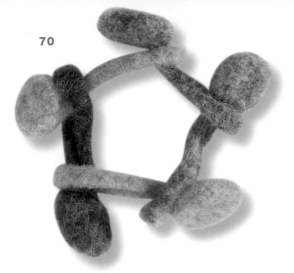

Perfect for beginners, this cute little bracelet is infinitely adjustable—make as many links as you like and work a necklace or belt to match. It looks best when each piece is worked in a different color.

LOOP'N'LINK **bracelet**

MAKING THE BRACELET

LINK (make 1 in each color)
Foundation ring: Ch 4 and join with sl st to form a ring.
Round 1: Ch 1, 8 sc in ring, join with sl st in first ch (8 sc).
Round 2: Ch 1, 2 sc in each sc around, join with sl st in first ch (16 sc).
Rounds 3–5: Ch 1, 1 sc in each sc around, join with sl st in first ch.
Round 6: Ch 1, sc2tog to end of round, join with sl st in first ch (8 sc).
Fasten off.

LOOP (make 1 in each color)
Foundation ring: Ch 20 and join with sl st to form a ring.
Round 1: Ch 1, into ring work 5 sl st, 5 dc, 5 hdc, 5 sc, 5 sl st.
Fasten off, leaving a 6" (15cm) tail.

FINISHING
For each loop, thread a tapestry needle with the tail of yarn and sew together the slip stitches. Sew the loop to the corresponding colored link. Weave in all ends, then felt. Link each piece together as shown in photo.

Skill level
Easy

Materials
• Hook: steel, size 4 (2mm)
• Yarn: 6½yds (6m) each of cream, orange, green, purple, blue, and pink sportweight wool
• Notions: tapestry needle

Finished size
Each felted link = 2¼" (6cm) long

See also
Felting, page 118

Abbreviations
ch—chain
dc—double crochet
hdc—half double crochet
sc—single crochet
sc2tog—single crochet 2 together (1 stitch decreased)
sl st—slip stitch

MAKING THE BRACELET

Mix up the beads and thread them onto the wire in a random color order; the first bead you thread onto the wire will be the last bead you use. **Foundation chain:** Ch 30, then [1 bch, ch 1] until all the beads are used, then ch 30. Fasten off.

FINISHING

Hold both ends of the crocheted chain together, folding in half. Place a pencil through both pieces at the fold and twist so that the chains twist around each other to form a tightly twisted cord. Remove the pencil to leave an open loop; twist the wire at the base of this open loop to form a secure fastening loop that will fit over the large bead. Thread the large bead onto the other end of the crocheted chain. Bend the excess chain around the large bead, then wrap it around the chain below the bead to secure the bead in place.

Tools and materials
- Hook: size C–2 (2.75mm)
- Wire: 11yds (10m) 28-gauge (0.3mm) gold wire
- Beads: 58 brightly colored 3mm beads; 14mm long oval bead
- Notions: pencil

Finished size
8" (20cm) long

Twister BRACELET

Skill level
Easy

Quick and easy to make, this pretty beaded bracelet will dress up any outfit—using lots of different bead colors makes it very adaptable. Make a matching choker by working a longer chain.

Abbreviations
bch—beaded chain
ch—chain
[ ]—work step in brackets number of times indicated

See also
Beaded crochet, page 38
Wire crochet, page 39

The use of pure wool tapestry yarn makes the petals on these flowers curl, giving them a natural look. The center of each flower is highlighted with pretty beads. You could make the bracelet using any combination of flower designs, or even a single flower design if you prefer.

CHUNKY flower bracelet

Skill level
Intermediate

Tools and materials

- Hook: size B–1 (2.25mm)
- Yarn: 11yd (10m) skeins of tapestry wool in 4 colors—2 skeins purple (A), 2 skeins lavender (B), 2 skeins light blue (C), 1 skein lime green (D)
- Beads: 29 purple 4mm beads; 12 frosted gold 4mm beads
- Notions: tapestry needle; ⅝" (15mm) shank button; dressmaking pins

Finished size

8¼" (21cm) long x 2¼" (5.5cm) at widest point

Abbreviations

ch—chain
dc—double crochet
fpsc—front post single crochet
hdc—half double crochet
RS—right side
sc—single crochet
sc2tog—single crochet 2 together (1 stitch decreased)
sl st—slip stitch
sp(s)—space(s)
WS—wrong side
[ ]—work step in brackets number of times indicated
( )—work step in parentheses in indicated stitch

See also

Raised stitches, page 34
Sewing on beads and sequins, page 107

MAKING THE BRACELET

FLOWER 1 (make 1)

Foundation ring: Using C, ch 4 and join with sl st to form a ring.
Round 1: Ch 1, 5 sc in ring, join with sl st in first sc (5 sc).
Work the first petal as follows.
Row 1 (RS): Ch 1, 2 sc in first sc, turn.
Row 2 (WS): Ch 1, [2 sc in next sc] twice, turn (4 sc).
Row 3: Ch 1, [2 sc in next sc] 4 times, turn (8 sc).
Rows 4–5: Ch 1, 1 sc in each sc across, turn.
Row 6: Ch 1, sc2tog, 1 sc in each of next 4 sc, sc2tog, turn (6 sc).
Row 7: Ch 1, sc2tog, 1 sc in each of next 2 sc, sc2tog (4 sc).
Fasten off.
Work four more petals in the same way as the first, joining yarn into next sc of round 1 after previous petal, and working first row in same st as join.

FLOWER 2 (make 1)

Foundation ring: Using C, ch 4 and join with sl st to form a ring.
Round 1: Ch 1, 1 sc in ring, [ch 4, 1 sc in ring] 5 times, ch 4, join sl st in first sc (6 ch-4 sps).
Round 2: Ch 1, work (1 sc, 1 hdc, 2 dc, 1 hdc, 1 sc) in each ch-4 sp, join with sl st in first sc.
Fasten off.

FLOWER 3 (make 2)

Foundation ring: Using D, ch 5 and join with sl st to form a ring.
Round 1: Ch 1, 6 sc in ring, join sl st in first sc.
Round 2: [Ch 8, 1 sc in second ch from hook, continuing along ch, work 1 hdc, 1 dc in each of next 3 ch, 1 hdc, 1 sc, join with sl st in next sc of round 1] 6 times.
Fasten off.

FLOWER 4 (make 2)

Using B, work as for flower 2 but do not fasten off. Turn and continue as follows using yarn A.
Round 3 (WS): Ch 1, 1 fpsc worked around first sc of round 1, [ch 5, 1 fpsc worked around next sc of round 1] 5 times, ch 5, join with sl st in first fpsc, turn (6 ch-5 sps).
Round 4 (RS): Ch 1, work (1 sc, 1 hdc, 3 dc, 1 hdc, 1 sc) in each ch-5 sp, join with sl st in first sc.
Fasten off.

STRAP

Foundation row: Using B, ch 43.
Row 1: 1 sc in second ch from hook and in each ch across, turn (42 sc).
Row 2: Ch 1, 1 sc in each sc across, ch 8, join with sl st in first sc of row 1 to form a fastening loop, turn. 10 sc in ch-8 sp, join with sl st in last sc of row 2.
Fasten off.

FINISHING

With a tapestry needle, weave in all ends. Sew a button at the end of the strap opposite the fastening loop. Sew 6 gold beads to the center of each flower 4; sew 6 purple beads to the center of flower 2, then 8 purple beads to the center of each remaining flower. Pin the flowers onto the strap in the following order, starting from the button end: 2, 3, 4, 1, 3, 4. The flowers should jostle each other and overlap. When you are happy with the positions, sew on firmly using the same color yarn as each flower.

SHELL **cuff bracelet**

Skill level
Easy

This bracelet has quite a bit of stretch, so the sizes are approximate. Make the bracelet smaller or larger by adding or subtracting five stitches to the beginning chain. You may wear the bracelet with or without the elasticized bead band, and vice versa.

MAKING THE BRACELET

These directions are written for the small size, with changes for the large size in brackets. When there is only one number, work for both sizes.

Foundation ring: Using larger hook, ch 30 [35] and join with sl st to form a ring.

Round 1 (RS): Ch 1, 1 sc in same st as join and in each of next 3 ch; *ch 1, skip 1 ch, 1 sc in each of next 4 ch; repeat from * around, end with ch 1, skip last st, join with sl st in first ch, turn (6 [7] ch-1 sps).

Round 2: Do not chain. *4 dc (shell) in ch-1 sp, working in back loops of sc throughout, 1 sc tbl in each of next 4 sc; repeat from * around (6 [7] shells). Do not join. Turn.

Round 3: Ch 1, *1 sc tbl in each of first 4 sc, ch 1, pulling shell forward to work behind it, skip shell; repeat from * around, join with sl st in first ch, turn.

Rounds 4–8: Repeat rounds 2–3 twice, then round 2 once more. End last round by joining with sl st in base of shell.
Fasten off.

With RS facing, join yarn to foundation ch just to the right of the first shell made in round 2; ch 1, skip shell, sl st to ch to the left of shell, turn. Repeat rounds 2–8 above for second half of bracelet, working round 2 in unworked loops of foundation ch.
Fasten off.

BEAD BAND

Thread beads onto elastic (this can be done without a beading needle). Using smaller hook, work a sufficient number of bch so that bead band, when slightly stretched, fits around the groove in the cuff bracelet. Join with sl st to form a ring. Fasten off.

FINISHING

With a tapestry needle, weave in all ends. Place bead band around center of bracelet.

Tools and materials
- Hook: size G–6 (4mm); size E–4 (3.5mm)
- Yarn: 90yds (83m) gold sportweight rayon metallic yarn
- Beads: 50 size 6º seed beads to match yarn
- Notions: lightweight beading elastic in matching color; tapestry needle

Finished size
Small [Large]
Small = to fit 5½–6½" (14–16.5cm) circumference wrist
Large = to fit 7–8" (18–20cm) circumference wrist

Abbreviations
bch—beaded chain
ch—chain
dc—double crochet
RS—right side
sc—single crochet
sl st—slip stitch
sp(s)—space(s)
st(s)—stitch(es)
tbl—through back loop

See also
Beaded crochet, page 38

REMINDER: WORKING THE SHELL PATTERN

1 In round 1, working a chain stitch, then skipping a foundation chain stitch, creates the chain spaces for working the shells in the next round.

2 In round 2, work 4 double crochet stitches in each chain space to create the shells.

3 Work round 3 behind the shells so that they become slightly raised at the front of the bracelet.

4 Join the yarn to the other side of the foundation ring to work a symmetrical shell pattern in the other direction.

5 Work the shell pattern as before, working into the unworked loops of the foundation ring for the first round of shells.

Skill level
Easy

The end of a watch strap often comes long before the clock fails to keep good time. Instead of buying a new strap, try making something more individual. Don't stop with the ideas shown here; add a semicircle of beads as shown in the denim earrings on pages 96–98, or make each shape in a different yarn or color.

DENIM **watch straps**

MAKING THE WATCH STRAPS

BEADED STRAP 1

Foundation ring: Using larger hook and A, ch 5, place bead onto hook, insert hook into first ch, yo, draw yarn through both loops and bead on hook, ch 5, join with sl st in first ch to form a ring. Two strands of yarn will appear either side of the bead; ensure they are next to the foundation chain.

Round 1: Ch 3 (counts as 1 dc), 8 dc in ring enclosing one strand of yarn, 9 dc in ring on other side of bead enclosing second strand of yarn, join with sl st in top of beg ch-3 (18 dc).
Fasten off.

Tier 1

Row 1: With WS facing and a new length of yarn, insert hook into rev lp of eighth st of previous round, yo, draw through, ch 7, skip 2 sts, sl st in rev lp of next st, turn.

Row 2: Ch 3, 9 dc in ch-7 sp (10 dc).
Fasten off.

Tier 2

Row 1: With WS facing and a new length of yarn, insert hook into rev lp of fourth st of previous row, yo, draw through, ch 5, skip 2 sts, sl st in rev lp of next st, turn.

Row 2: Repeat row 2 of tier 1.
Fasten off.

Tongue

Change to smaller hook and use a split length of A (see notes overleaf).

Row 3: With WS facing, insert hook into rev lp of fourth st of previous row, yo, draw through, ch 3, 1 dc in rev lp of each of next 3 sts, turn.

Row 4: Ch 3, 1 dc in each st across, turn (4 dc). Repeat row 4 until the length of strap measures 5½" (14cm) from center of watch face.

Next row: Ch 3, dcdec. Fasten off.

Tools and materials

- Hook: size C–2 (2.75mm); steel, size 10 (1.3mm)
- Yarn: 15yds (14m) each of cream (A) and blue (B) DK-weight denim cotton yarn
- Beads: 2 color-lined 8mm round glass accent beads (beaded strap only); make sure the hole in the beads is large enough to accommodate the hook
- Findings: 1 watch face and 1 buckle per watch strap
- Notions: bleach; tapestry needle

Finished size

Whole circle motif = 1¼" (3cm) before washing
Blue strap = 1" (2.5cm) wide x 8¼" (21cm) long, including buckle
Beaded strap = 1¼" (3cm) wide x 9" (23cm) long, including buckle

Abbreviations

beg—begin(ning)
ch—chain
dc—double crochet
dcdec—*yo, insert hook in next st, yo, draw through, yo, draw through 2 loops on hook, repeat from * in each st on row, yo, draw through all loops on hook
rev lp(s)—reverse loop(s): horizontal bar(s) under the top stitch loops on WS
RS—right side
sl st—slip stitch
sp—space
st(s)—stitch(es)
WS—wrong side
yo—yarn over

REMINDER: INSERTING THE BEAD AND WORKING INTO REVERSE LOOPS

1 To insert the bead, work a chain, place the bead onto the hook, then join to the first ch st, pulling the yarn through the bead.

2 Work a chain around the other side of the bead, then join to the first chain stitch to form a ring.

3 Work double crochet around each side of the ring, enclosing the strands of yarn as you do so.

4 Start the tiers and tongue by attaching a new length of yarn in the specified reverse loop of the previous row.

5 Work a chain, then attach the chain to the specified reverse loop of the previous row. Complete the tiers and tongue as instructed.

(continues overleaf)

(continued from page 77)

Notes
- Split lengths of yarn have been used to sew the straps to the watch-face brackets, to crochet the loop at the buckle for the blue watch strap, and to crochet the narrow section of the beaded watch strap. Cut a 65" (165cm) length of A for beaded watch strap and a 12" (30cm) length of B for blue watch strap. Untwist strands and split each into two lengths.

- For a tighter round, put an extra dc at the end of the round 1 before fastening off.

BEADED STRAP 2
Work as for beaded strap 1 until row 2 of tier 2 has been completed. Fasten off.

BLUE STRAP 1
Foundation ring: Using larger hook and B, ch 10 and join with sl st to form a ring.
Round 1: Ch 3 (counts as 1 dc), 18 dc in ring, join with sl st in top of beg ch-3 (19 dc).
Fasten off.

Tier 1
Row 1: With WS facing and a new length of yarn, insert hook into rev lp of any st of previous round, yo, draw through, ch 5, skip 1 st, sl st in rev lp of next st, turn.
Row 2 (RS): Ch 3 (counts as 1 dc), 10 dc in ch-5 sp (11 dc).
Fasten off.

Tier 2
Row 1: With WS facing and a new length of yarn, insert hook into rev lp of fifth st of previous row, yo, draw through, ch 5, skip 1 st, sl st in rev lp of fifth st, turn.
Row 2: Repeat row 2 of tier 1.
Fasten off.

Tongue
Row 3: With WS facing and a new length of yarn, insert hook into rev lp of the fifth st of previous row, yo, draw through, ch 3, 1 dc in rev lp of each of next 2 sts, turn (3 dc).
Row 4: Ch 3, 1 dc in each st across, turn (3 dc).
Repeat row 4 until the length of strap measures 5" (12.5cm) from center of watch face when edge of beg ring is on top of watch-face bracket.
Next row: Ch 3, dcdec.
Fasten off.

BLUE STRAP 2
Work as for blue strap 1 until row 2 of tier 2 has been completed. Fasten off.

FINISHING
Blue watch strap only
Place both straps into an old pillowcase and secure the opening. Wash on a 140–160°F (60–70°C) cycle and allow the straps to dry flat. There will be some dye loss, so wash with dark items that will not stain. Enhance the contours by brushing them with a diluted bleach solution and leaving for a period of time before washing again. Before putting bleach solution on watch straps, test on a piece of the same yarn to determine length of time to leave on before rinsing.

Both styles
Using a split length of yarn, overcast through the rev lps on round 1 of rings and the watch-face brackets; attach strap 1 to the bottom bracket and strap 2 to the top bracket. Overcast the buckle onto the other end of strap 2. On the blue watch strap only, make a loop at the base of the buckle over the front of the strap by using the smaller hook and inserting it into the back of the last st, yo, draw through, ch 10, sl st into the back of the st on the opposite side. Fasten off. With a tapestry needle, weave in all ends.

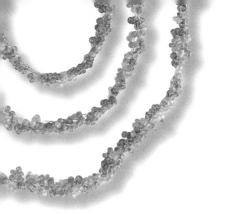

Loop this length of beaded chain around your wrist several times to wear it as a bracelet, or wear it as a single- or double-strand necklace. Put the reel of wire into a small drawstring bag, such as a little organza gift bag, to help keep the wire under control while working.

BEADED **chain bracelet**

MAKING THE BRACELET

Thread beads onto wire, alternating 5 A beads and 5 B beads.

Row 1: Leaving a 4" (10cm) tail, make a slipknot and ch 1 to start. Being careful not to work too tightly, work 38" (96.5cm) of bch, bringing up 5 beads for each chain stitch, ending with opposite color of beginning, ch 1, do not turn.

Row 2: Working back along the chain, loosely work a sl st into each ch of row 1, bringing up 5 beads for each sl st.
Cut wire, leaving an 8" (20cm) tail. Insert hook into the first ch at the beginning of the bracelet, and holding both the beginning and ending wire ends together, work 2 sc into beginning ch.

FINISHING

Wrap both ends of the wire firmly around the join several times, then thread each end separately down through several sets of beads, then back up through several different sets. Cut wire close to last bead.

Skill level
Intermediate

Tools and materials
- Hook: size D–3 (3.25mm)
- Wire: 24yd (22m) reel of 32-gauge (0.2mm) silver wire
- Beads: ¾oz (20g) size 11º seed bead mix (A); ¾oz (20g) size 11º seed bead mix in a contrasting color scheme (B)

Finished size
38" (96.5cm) long before joining into a circle

See also
Beaded crochet, page 38
Wire crochet, page 39

Abbreviations
bch—beaded chain	sc—single crochet
ch—chain	sl st—slip stitch

Using the same basic bangle, different looks are obtained by varying the embellishments. A zigzag line of surface crochet is interspersed with pretty flower accent beads on one bangle, while the other is finished with crocheted flower motifs.

FRILLY **floral bangles**

Skill level
Intermediate

Tools and materials
Beaded bangle
- Hook: size C–2 (2.75mm)
- Thread/yarn: 40yds (37m) black fingering-weight crochet cotton or embroidery thread (A); 40yds (37m) blue metallic yarn (B)
- Beads: 11–12 small glass flower beads; 11–12 size 11° seed beads
- Notions: tapestry needle; ½" (15mm) silver button

Motif bangle
- Hook: size C–2 (2.75mm)
- Thread/wire: 40yds (37m) gold rayon thread (A); 2yds (2m) 32-gauge (0.2mm) black wire (B); 2yds (2m) red mercerized crochet cotton (C)
- Notions: tapestry needle; ½" (15mm) red button

Finished size
¾" (2cm) wide x wrist measurement plus ¾" (2cm) long

Abbreviations
beg—begin(ning)
ch—chain
dc—double crochet
hdc—half double crochet
lp(s)—loop(s)
sc—single crochet
sl st—slip stitch
st(s)—stitch(es)

See also
Surface crochet, page 36
Wire crochet, page 39
Sewing on beads and sequins, page 107

MAKING THE BANGLES

BEADED BANGLE
Foundation chain: Using A, ch 5.
Row 1: 1 sc in second ch from hook and in each ch across, turn (4 sc).
Row 2: Ch 1, 1 sc in each sc across, turn.
Repeat row 2 until piece measures the same as your wrist plus ¾" (2cm).
Ch 6 or 7, join with sl st to beginning of row to make fastening loop.
Fasten off. With a tapestry needle, weave in all ends. Join B to top right-hand corner of strap (loop end) and work a zigzag line of surface crochet evenly along the bracelet.
Work ch 1 over the edge so that thread is now at the top of the work, turn.
Next row: Ch 3 (counts as 1 dc), working under both loops of the surface crochet, work 5 dc in first st, 6 dc in each st to end.
Fasten off.

FINISHING
With a tapestry needle, weave in all ends. Sew one flower bead topped with one seed bead in each "V" created by the zigzag row. Sew button to opposite end from loop for closure.

MOTIF BANGLE
Using A, work the base band as for the beaded bangle (do not embellish with surface crochet).

Wire flower
Foundation ring: Using B, ch 4 and join with sl st to form a ring.
Round 1: Ch 1, 10 sc in ring, join with sl st in first sc.
Round 2: Ch 2 (counts as 2 hdc), 1 hdc in same st as join, 2 hdc in each st around, join with sl st in top of beg ch-2 (20 hdc).
Round 3: Ch 2, 3 hdc in same st as join, 4 hdc in each st around, join with sl st in top of beg ch-2 (80 hdc).
Fasten off.

Cotton flower
Foundation ring: Using C, ch 3 and join with sl st to form a ring.
Round 1: Ch 1, 10 sc in ring, join with sl st in first sc.
Round 2: *Ch 4, sl st in next st, repeat from * around (10 ch-4 lps).
Fasten off.

FINISHING
With a tapestry needle, weave in all ends. Sew the wire flower to center of base band, then sew the cotton flower on top. Sew button to opposite end from loop for closure.

ORGANIC **bracelet**

Skill level
Easy

This unusual-shaped bracelet is embellished with a beaded fringe. The selection of beads and their position in the fringe is entirely your own choice, so the bracelet will be your own "one-off" design. The use of flexible wire for the fringe helps it to keep its position alongside the felted extensions while allowing some movement for comfort, but you could use beading thread for a more flexible result.

MAKING THE BRACELET

Foundation chain: Ch 3.
Row 1: 1 sc in second ch from hook and in next ch, turn (2 sc).
Rows 2–7: Ch 1, 1 sc in each of next 2 sc, turn.
Row 8: Ch 7, 1 sc in second ch from hook and in each st across, turn (8 sc).
Rows 9–10: Repeat row 2 twice (2 sc).
Row 11: Ch 4, 1 sc in second ch from hook and in each st across, turn (5 sc).
Rows 12–13: Repeat row 2 twice (2 sc).
Row 14: Ch 5, 1 sc in second ch from hook and in each st across, turn (6 sc).
Rows 15–20: Repeat row 2 six times (2 sc).
Row 21: Ch 6, 1 sc in second ch from hook and in each st across, turn (7 sc).
Rows 22–27: Repeat row 2 six times (2 sc).
Row 28: Ch 7, 1 sc in second ch from hook and in each st across, turn (8 sc).
Rows 29–30: Repeat row 2 twice (2 sc).
Row 31: Ch 3, 1 sc in second ch from hook and in each st across, turn (4 sc).
Rows 32–39: Repeat row 2 eight times (2 sc). Fasten off.

FINISHING

With a tapestry needle, weave in all ends, then felt. Sew the beaded fringe along each side of the bracelet using wire or thread and a beading needle; the exact arrangement of beads is not important, but starting with bugle beads and placing larger beads at the end of each fringe looks best. The exact placement of the fringes is not important either; just aim for a reasonably symmetrical result. Sew a button at one end of the bracelet. Mark where the buttonhole should be on the opposite end and cut a small slit. It is best to cut the buttonhole slightly smaller than the button because the fabric will stretch to fit.

Tools and materials
- Hook: size M–13 (9mm)
- Yarn: 45yds (41m) red super bulky-weight wool
- Beads: about 85 brightly colored bugle, seed, and other glass beads
- Notions: tapestry needle; 1yd (1m) flexible jewelry wire, beading wire, or beading thread; beading needle; 1" (25mm) button

Finished size
About 10½" (27cm) long, depending on how much bracelet is felted
Center band = 1" (2.5cm) wide excluding fringe

Abbreviations
ch—chain
sc—single crochet
st(s)—stitch(es)

See also
External increases, page 32
Felting, page 118

REMINDER: ADDING A FRINGE

   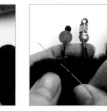

1 Secure the thread or wire in the felted bracelet at the first fringe position with a few small stitches.

2 Thread on the beads in the desired arrangement. End with a small bead.

3 Skipping the small bead, take the needle back up through all the other beads and into the bracelet.

4 Move the needle through the felted piece to the next fringe position. Add beads, then take the wire to the next fringe position.

5 Continue in this way to complete the fringe. Secure the end of the thread or wire with a few small stitches. Trim close to the felted piece.

This delicate beaded bracelet can easily be crocheted in a single evening. Worked in a fine yet durable gold wire and threaded with a mixture of beads in different colors and sizes, the single crochet stitch design looks far more complicated than it really is.

DELICATE **beaded bracelet**

MAKING THE BRACELET

*Thread 3–4 small beads and then 1 medium bead onto the wire; repeat from *, alternating the colors to give a random effect. Remember that the first bead you thread on will be the last bead worked.

Foundation chain: Ch 37.

Row 1: 1 sc in each of next 2 sts, 1 bsc in next st, *1 sc in next st, 1 bsc in next st; repeat from * 14 more times, 1 sc in each of next 3 sts, turn (36 sts).

Row 2: Ch 1, 1 sc in each st across, turn. Fine wire can be difficult to work with if you are not used to it, but don't worry if you do not work each stitch in the exact place because this will just add to the random feel of the piece. All that is important is that you have the correct number of stitches.

Rows 3–4: Repeat rows 1–2.

Row 5: Repeat row 1. Fasten off.

FINISHING

Using wire, sew the clasp and jump ring to opposite ends of the bracelet. Wrap the ends of the wire around the join and press in the ends neatly.

Skill level
Intermediate

Tools and materials
- Hook: steel, size 6 (1.8mm)
- Wire: 24yd (22m) reel of 32-gauge (0.2mm) gold wire
- Beads: 10 medium and 12 small lime green beads; 15 small dark green beads; 15 small metallic gray beads
- Findings: 1 gold clasp and jump ring
- Notions: beading needle

Finished size
7½" (19cm) long

See also
Beaded crochet, page 38
Wire crochet, page 39
Fastenings and findings, pages 46–47

Abbreviations
bsc—beaded single crochet
ch—chain
sc—single crochet
st(s)—stitch(es)

MAKING THE BRACELET

Measure the wrist. Using wire, work a chain about 1–1½" (2.5–4cm) smaller than this measurement, rounding the number of chains to a multiple of 2.

Row 1: 1 sc in second ch from hook, *ch 1, skip 1 ch, 1 sc in front loop of next ch*; repeat from * across, turn.

Row 2: Ch 1, 1 sc in first sc, *ch 1, skip 1 st, 1 sc in next sc; repeat from * across, turn.
Repeat row 2 until piece measures about 1¼" (3cm) from beginning.
Fasten off.

Join the crochet thread to the wire piece and continue working in rounds around the wire piece as follows.

Round 1: Ch 1, 1 sc in each st around, adjusting so total sts are a multiple of 3; join with sl st in first ch.

Round 2: *Ch 3, skip 2 sc, sl st in next sc; repeat from * around, join with sl st in first ch.

Round 3: Work (1 sc, 1 hdc, 3 dc, 1 hdc, 1 sc) in each ch-3 sp around, join with sl st in first sc.
Fasten off.

Tools and materials

• Hook: steel, size 8 (1.5mm)

• Wire/thread/yarn: 24yd (22m) reel of 24-gauge (0.5mm) non-tarnish sterling silver wire; 45yds (41m) pink laceweight nylon crochet thread; small amount of blue novelty yarn for the cord

Finished size

Cobweb panel is 5" (12.5cm) long x 2" (5cm) wide
Total length is adjustable

Cobweb BRACELET

Skill level
Intermediate

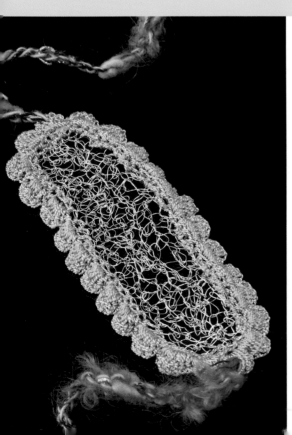

FINISHING

Attach the novelty yarn to the center of one end of the bracelet and work ch until desired length is reached. Fasten off. Repeat at the other end, making sure that both cords are long enough to tie a bow to fasten the bracelet around the wrist.

This is a great bracelet to make as a gift because it fastens with a simple cord, so the size is adjustable. Choose different color combinations of yarn and wire to suit the person it is for. You could also make a matching choker by working a longer centerpiece.

Abbreviations

ch—chain
dc—double crochet
hdc—half double crochet
sc—single crochet
sl st—slip stitch
sp—space
st(s)—stitch(es)
( )—work step in parentheses in indicated stitch

See also
Wire crochet, page 39

This exotic bangle works up fast from two hairpin crochet strips. Pair it with other bangles in your collection for an eclectic look. The beads used here harmonize beautifully with the copper wire, but you could use a contrasting color if you prefer.

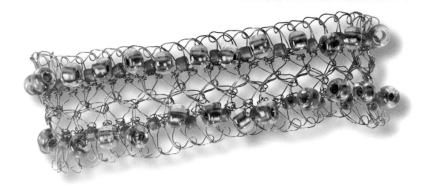

HAIRPIN **wire bangle**

MAKING THE BANGLE

For each strip, thread the beads onto the wire in the following sequence: [A, B] 24 times.

Work strips (make 2): Set loom to 1½" (4cm) and use a twisted loop on the starting pin instead of a slipknot. Catch a bead in every other stitch of the hairpin strip; they will align on one side (RS) of the strip only. Work 96 loops in total, then fasten off. Leave 6" (15cm) tails at beginning and end.

Make circle: Use the tails of each strip to weave the beginning and end of the strip together so that the strip now forms a cylinder, keeping the RS facing out. Assemble each cylindrical strip so that one is on top of the other, with the side of each strip closest to the beads facing out. Join the strips with a 2x2 cable join, using one of the wire tails to secure the last 2 loops of the join in cable join pattern. Work a cable heading at each edge of the bracelet, using tails to secure the last loop of each heading. Secure and trim all wire ends.

Tools and materials
- Hook: steel, size 7 (1.65mm)
- Hairpin loom
- Wire: 20yds (18m) 28-gauge (0.3mm) copper wire
- Beads: 48 red-lined 6mm dichroic glass seed beads (A); 48 opalescent orange size 6° glass seed beads (B)

Finished size
2½" (6.5cm) diameter; 4" (10cm) long when folded flat

Abbreviations
RS—right side
[ ]—work step in brackets number of times indicated

See also
Hairpin crochet, pages 40–41
Cable techniques, page 42

REMINDER: WORKING AND JOINING HAIRPIN STRIPS

1 To catch a bead in a stitch, wrap wire over hook, draw through, slide bead up to hook, wire over, and draw through again.

2 Continue in this way, catching a bead in every other stitch of the hairpin strip. Repeat for the second strip.

3 To work a 2x2 cable join, insert the hook through two loops of the first strip.

4 Insert the hook through two loops of the second strip.

5 Pull the second two loops through the first two. Carefully manipulate the wire to neaten the join as necessary.

This pretty watch strap could be just the start of a collection of jewelry pieces. Use the daisy motif and strap length to make a bracelet or necklace, or look through the book and use the daisy to replace motifs in other projects. Try working the flowers in different colors, and the addition of beads to the first round would add extra sparkle.

DAISY **watch strap**

MAKING THE WATCH STRAP

DAISY (make 5)

Round 1: Using A, ch 4 (counts as 1 dc, 1 ch), work 7 dc in first ch, join with sl st in top of beg ch-3 (8 dc).

Round 2: Ch 1, 1 sc tbl of same st as join and in each dc around, join with sl st in first ch.
Fasten off A.

Round 3: Using B, insert hook tbl of top of first sc, yo, draw through, make petal, sl st into base of ch, *make petal, sl st tbl of next sc, make petal, sl st in same sc; repeat from * around, finishing with sl st in last sc (16 petals).
Fasten off B.

STRAP 1

Using C, *insert hook through bottom watch-face bracket, yo, draw loop through bracket, yo from outside of bracket, draw through all loops on hook, repeat from * 6 more times, turn (7 sc).

Row 1: Ch 4 (counts as 1 dc, 1 ch), skip 1 st, 1 sc in next st, ch 1, skip 1 st, 1 dc in next st, ch 1, skip 1 st, 1 sc in last st.

Row 2: Ch 4 (counts as 1 dc, 1 ch), skip 1 st, 1 sc in next dc, skip 1 st, 1 dc in next sc, skip 1 st, 1 sc in third ch of beg ch-4.
Repeat row 2 an even number of times until strap measures 5" (12.5cm) from center of watch face.

Next row: Ch 2, *1 sc in ch-1 sp, 1 sc in next st; repeat from * across.
Fasten off.

STRAP 2

On top watch-face bracket, work as for strap 1 until strap measures 3¼" (8cm) from center of watch face.

FINISHING

Complete the flowers by pulling the thread A ends tight and weaving the thread B ends around the base of round 3. Pull firmly before securing all the ends. Complete the straps by sewing the buckle to the end of strap 2. Make a loop at the base of the buckle over the front of the strap by using C and inserting the hook into the back of the last st, yo, draw through, ch 17, sl st into the back of st on the opposite side. Insert hook under the ch and work 17 sc across. Fasten off. With a tapestry needle, weave in all ends of thread C through the sc sts. Sew the flowers to the straps, slightly overlapping the watch face and adjacent flowers; attach three on strap 1 and two on strap 2.

Tools and materials
- Hook: steel, size 6 (1.8mm)
- Thread: 5yds (4.5m) yellow embroidery cotton (A); 9yds (8m) each of white (B) and green (C) embroidery cotton
- Findings: watch face and buckle
- Notions: tapestry needle

Finished size
Strap = 9¼" (23.5cm) long including buckle
Daisies = 1⅜" (3.5cm) diameter

Abbreviations
beg—begin(ning)
ch—chain
dc—double crochet
make petal—ch 6, then sl st in each ch back along length of ch
sc—single crochet
sl st—slip stitch
sp—space
st(s)—stitch(es)
tbl—through back loop
yo—yarn over

See also
Fastenings and findings, pages 46–47

CHAPTER 4

Earrings

Earrings are ideal for using up tiny scraps of yarn and leftover beads. Designs include playful snowmen and circle earrings, as well as stunning chandelier drops and sparkly crosses.

The denim earrings project features six fabulous variations, showing how a single design idea can be adapted to make a range of different styles.

SNOWMEN **earrings**

Skill level
Intermediate

These earrings are a lot of fun both to crochet and to wear. They also make a unique seasonal gift for friends and family. Experiment with different yarns and colors for the hat and the scarf. You could also "dress" the head and body in other ways to create a whole host of fun earring motifs, from teddy bears and pandas to dolls and fairies.

MAKING THE EARRINGS (make 2 of each piece)

HEAD AND BODY

Foundation ring: Using A, ch 6 and join with sl st to form a ring.

Round 1: Ch 1, 9 sc in ring, join with sl st in first ch.

Round 2: Ch 1, 2 sc in each sc around, join with sl st in first ch (18 sc).

Slip a small bead inside the crochet and continue.

Rounds 3–5: Ch 1, 1 sc in each sc around, join with sl st in first ch.

Round 6: Ch 1, *1 sc in each of next 4 sc, sc2tog; repeat from * around, join with sl st in first ch (15 sc).

Round 7: Ch 1, *2 sc in each of next 2 sc, 1 sc in next sc; repeat from * around to last 3 sc, 2 sc in each of next 3 sc, join with sl st in first ch (26 sc).

Rounds 8–9: Repeat round 3.

Round 10: Ch 1, [1 sc in each of next 12 sc, 2 sc in next sc] twice, join with sl st in first ch (28 sc).

Slip a large bead inside the crochet and continue.

Rounds 11–12: Ch 1, [sc2tog] around, join with sl st in first ch (7 sc at end of round 12).

Round 13: Ch 1, [sc2tog] 3 times, 1 sc in last sc, join with sl st in first ch (4 sc).

Round 14: Ch 1, [sc2tog] twice, join with sl st in first ch. Fasten off.

HAT AND SCARF

Foundation ring: Using B, ch 6 and join with sl st to form a ring.

Round 1: Ch 1, 8 sc in ring, join with sl st in first ch (8 sc).

Round 2: Ch 1, 1 sc in each sc around, join with sl st in first ch.

Round 3: Ch 1, 2 sc in each sc around, join with sl st in first ch (16 sc).

Round 4: Ch 1, [1 sc in each of next 7 sc, 2 sc in next sc] twice, join with sl st in first ch (18 sc). Fasten off.

To make the scarf, ch 35 using C. Fasten off.

FINISHING

Using a tapestry needle, weave in all ends. For each earring, sew a hat onto the snowman's head using B. Tie the scarf around the neck and use the crochet hook or tapestry needle to push the ends inside to hide them and to attach scarf ends to body. Using black thread, sew a couple of stitches on the snowman's head for each eye. Twist open the loop of an ear wire, attach it to the top of the hat, then twist the loop securely closed.

Tools and materials

- Hook: steel, size 8 (1.5mm)
- Thread: 32yds (30m) white laceweight nylon crochet thread (A); small amounts of red (B) and green (C) crochet thread
- Beads: 2 white or clear 15mm glass beads; 2 white or clear 18mm glass beads
- Findings: 2 ear wires
- Notions: tapestry needle; sewing needle and black thread

Finished size

1½" (4cm) long

Abbreviations

ch—chain
sc—single crochet
sc2tog—single crochet 2 together (1 stitch decreased)
sl st—slip stitch
[ ]—work step in brackets number of times indicated

See also

Fastenings and findings, pages 46–47
Crocheting around beads, page 51

REMINDER: BUILDING A SNOWMAN

1 Work rounds 1–6 around the small bead for the head, then increase the crochet to fit the large bead.

2 Crochet around the large bead to complete the body of the snowman, then weave in the ends.

3 Sew the hat with small, neat stitches to the top of the snowman's head.

4 Tie the scarf around the neck, then push the ends inside to secure, making them different lengths.

5 Add a couple of small stitches for each eye, on the front of the head above where the scarf is tied.

These earrings are very quick to work up with crochet or embroidery thread and store-bought hoops. You could use a third color for rows 4 and 5 if you prefer, and opt for either subtle toning shades or brightly contrasting ones.

HOOP **earrings**

MAKING THE EARRINGS (make 2)

Foundation chain: Using A, ch 41.
Row 1: 1 hsc in second ch from hook and in each ch to end, turn (40 sts).
Without breaking off A, join B.
Row 2: Using B, ch 1, [sc2tog, 1 sc in each of next 6 sts] across, turn (35 sts).
Row 3: Ch 1, [sc2tog, 1 sc in each of next 5 sts] across, turn (30 sts).
Break off B and continue using A.
Row 4: Ch 1, [sc2tog, 1 sc in each of next 4 sts] across, turn (25 sts).
Row 5: Ch 1, [sc2tog, 1 sc in each of next 3 sts, picot] 4 times, sc2tog, 1 sc in each of next 3 sts (20 sts).
Fasten off.

FINISHING
With a tapestry needle, weave in all ends.

Skill level
Intermediate

Tools and materials
- Hook: steel, size 5 (1.9mm)
- Thread: 12yds (11m) each of beige (A) and orange (B) embroidery cotton
- Findings: two 2½" (6.5cm) diameter earring hoops
- Notions: tapestry needle

Finished size
2½" (6.5cm) diameter, but depends on size of hoops

See also
Crocheting around hoops or rings, page 37

Abbreviations
ch—chain
hsc—hoop single crochet
picot—ch 3, then sl st to first of ch-3
sc—single crochet
sc2tog—single crochet 2 together (1 stitch decreased)
st(s)—stitch(es)
[ ]—work step in brackets number of times indicated

MAKING THE EARRINGS

SMALL CIRCLE (make 8: 4 A, 4 B)
Foundation ring: Using A, ch 4 and join with sl st to form a ring.
Round 1: Ch 1, 10 sc in ring (10 sc).
Round 2: Ch 1, 2 sc in same st as join and in each sc around, join with sl st in first sc (20 sc).
Round 3: Ch 1, 1 sc in same st as join, 2 sc in next sc, *1 sc in next sc, 2 sc in next sc; repeat from * around, join with sl st in first ch (30 sc).
Fasten off.
Repeat to make three more circles in A, then four circles in B.

LARGE CIRCLE (make 4: 2 A, 2 B)
Work as for small circle through round 3, but do not fasten off.
Round 4. Ch 1, 1 sc in same st as join and in next sc, 2 sc in next sc, *1 sc in each of next 2 sc, 2 sc in next sc; repeat from * around, join with sl st in first sc (40 sc).
Round 5: Ch 1, 1 sc in same st as join and in each of next 2 sc, 2 sc in next sc, *1 sc in each of next 3 sc, 2 dc in next sc; repeat from * around, join with sl st in first ch (50 sts).
Fasten off.
Repeat to make another circle in A, then two circles in B.

Tools and materials
- Hook: steel, size 8 (1.5mm)
- Thread: 45yds (41m) each of pink (A) and yellow (B) laceweight nylon crochet thread; small amount of blue (C) crochet thread
- Findings: 2 ear wires
- Notions: tapestry needle

Finished size
3½" (9cm) long excluding ear wire x 1¼" (3cm) at widest point

Circle EARRINGS

Skill level
Intermediate

FINISHING
With a tapestry needle, sew pairs of A and B circles together using thread C around the edge, referring to photo as a guide. Use large stitches that extend across the outer rounds of the circles. Sew sets of three double-sided circles together, with two small ones at the top and a large one at the bottom. Weave in all ends. Attach an ear wire to the top of each earring.

These playful earrings are made in two main colors, but you could make each circle in a different color for even bigger impact. Adapt them by finishing the circles a row early for a smaller pair of earrings, or by adding beads to the circle centers for a party look.

Abbreviations
ch—chain
dc—double crochet
sc—single crochet
sl st—slip stitch
st(s)—stitch(es)

See also
Fastenings and findings, pages 46–47

Each of these six pairs of earrings only requires a tiny amount of yarn, so make them to complement other home-worked projects by using up leftover yarn. Use either the main color of the other project or select a keynote color, which will give a more subtle focal point. The four smaller variations are for earrings that sit just on the ear or have only a short drop, keeping the focus high on the neck.

DENIM **earrings**

MAKING THE EARRINGS (make 2 of each)

TWO-TIER SEMICIRCLE EARRINGS
Circle motif
Round 1: Using A, ch 4 (counts as 1 dc, 1 ch), 12 dc in fourth ch from hook, changing to B at end of last dc, join with sl st in top of beg ch, do not turn (13 dc).
Round 2: Using B, ch 3 (counts as 1 dc), 1 dc in same st as join, 2 dc in each st around (26 dc). Fasten off.

Tier 1
Row 1: With WS facing and a new length of B, insert hook into rev lp of any dc of last round, yo, draw through, ch 7, skip 2 dc, sl st in rev lp of next dc, turn.
Row 2 (RS): Ch 3 (counts as 1 dc), 13 dc in ch-7 sp (14 dc).
Fasten off.

Tier 2
Row 1: Thread the beads onto a new length of B and, with WS facing, insert hook into rev lp of sixth dc, yo, draw through, ch 7, skip 2 dc, sl st in rev lp of next dc, turn.
Row 2: Ch 3 (counts as 1 dc), *pb, 2 dc in ch-7 sp; repeat from * 5 more times, pb, 1 dc in ch-7 sp (14 dc).
Fasten off.

BEADED FRINGE EARRINGS
Work as for two-tier semicircle earrings through end of tier 1. Fasten off.
Row 2: With RS facing and C, insert hook into rev lp of fourth st of tier 1, yo, draw through, ch 3 (counts as 1 dc), 1 dc in same st as join; working into rev lp of each st, work [1 dc in next st, 2 dc in next st] twice, 2 dc in next st, 1 dc in next st, 2 dc in next st (13 dc).
Fasten off.
Row 3: With RS facing and 6" (15cm) lengths of A, insert hook into rev lp of fourth st of last row, yo, draw through, ch 3 (counts as 1 dc), 1 dc in same st as join, *1 dc in rev lp of next st (join a new length of A before completing the stitch), 2 dc in rev lp of next st, repeat from * twice more (11 dc).
Fasten off.
Using a tapestry needle, weave in the beginning of each length of last row and pass the end lengths under the rev lp of the corresponding sts.
For the outer end lengths, use a tapestry needle and thread [1 large blue bead, 1 gold bead] 3 times, then 1 small blue bead onto the yarn. Push the beads up until they sit firmly against the sts of row 3. Skip the small blue bead and pass the needle back through the other beads. Weave in the end securely. For the center length, thread [1 large blue, 1 gold, 1 red, 1 gold bead] twice, then 1 large blue, 1 gold, 1 small blue bead onto the yarn. Skip the small blue bead and continue as for the outer lengths.

FINISHING (both styles)
Weave in all ends and finish each circular motif by threading the ends under both top loops of the first stitch of the last round and back through the center of the last stitch worked. Weave in on the WS to secure. Attach the earring findings.

Tools and materials
Two-tier semicircle earrings
- Hook: steel, size 10 (1.3mm)
- Yarn: 1yd (1m) red sportweight cotton yarn (A); 10ft (3m) blue DK-weight denim cotton yarn (B)
- Beads: 14 red 3mm miracle beads
- Findings: 2 ear posts and 2 ear nuts
- Notions: tapestry needle

Beaded fringe earrings
- Hook: steel, size 8 (1.25mm)
- Yarn/thread: 1yd (1m) red sportweight cotton yarn (A); 5ft (1.5m) blue DK-weight denim cotton yarn (B); 1yd (1m) yellow embroidery cotton (C)
- Beads: 18 blue 3mm plastic beads; 22 gold 2mm glass beads; 6 blue 1mm plastic beads; 4 red 4mm glass beads
- Findings: 2 ear posts and 2 ear nuts
- Notions: tapestry needle

Four smaller variations
Adapt materials and tools for the two-tier semicircle earrings as necessary

Finished size
Large round motif = 1" (2.5cm) diameter
Two-tier semicircle earrings = 1" (2.5cm) wide x 2" (5cm) long
Beaded fringe earrings = 1" (2.5cm) wide x 3" (7.5cm) long

(continues overleaf)

98

(continued from page 97)

Abbreviations
beg—begin(ning)
ch—chain
dc—double crochet
pb—place bead: slide bead along
yarn to base of loop on the hook
rev lp—reverse loop: horizontal bar
under the top stitch loops on WS
RS—right side
sl st—slip stitch
sp—space
st(s)—stitch(es)
WS—wrong side
yo—yarn over
[ ]—work step in brackets
number of times indicated

See also
Beaded crochet, page 38
Fastenings and findings,
pages 46–47

Notes
The motifs have been crocheted using
split lengths of yarn. Cut 33" (84cm)
lengths of A, then untwist and split into
one three-strand length and one two-
strand length. Cut 56" (142cm) lengths
of B, then untwist and split into two
three-strand lengths.

VARIATIONS

HALF-CIRCLE EARRINGS
Work rounds 1 and 2 as for the two-tier semicircle
earrings, but only work 14 dc in round 2 before
fastening off.

THREE-QUARTER CIRCLE EARRINGS
Work rounds 1 and 2 as for the two-tier semicircle
earrings, but only work 20 dc in round 2 before
fastening off.

BEADED HALF-CIRCLE EARRINGS
Thread 7 beads onto B and work round 1 as for the
two-tier semicircle earrings.
Round 2: Using B, ch 2, pb, 1 dc in same st as
join, *1 dc in next dc, pb, 1 dc in same st, repeat
from * 5 more times. Fasten off.

ONE-TIER SEMICIRCLE EARRINGS
Thread 7 beads onto B and work through round 2 of
the two-tier semicircle earrings, then work tier 2.
Fasten off.

MAKING THE EARRINGS (make 4 pieces)

Foundation chain: Ch 4.
Row 1: 1 sc in second ch from hook and in each ch across, turn (3 sc).
Row 2: Ch 1, 1 sc in each sc across, turn.
Row 3: Ch 1, 1 sc in each sc across, ch 4, turn.
Row 4: 1 sc in second ch from hook and in each ch and sc across, remove the hook. Insert the hook into the same sc as one just worked, ch 3, fasten off. Insert the hook back into the loop from last sc, then work 1 sc in each ch, turn (9 sc).
Rows 5–6: Ch 1, 1 sc in each sc across, turn. Fasten off at end of row 6.

Row 7: Skip 3 sc, join the yarn to the next sc, ch 1, 1 sc in same st as join and in each of next 2 sc, turn (3 sc).
Row 8: Ch 1, 1 sc in each sc across. Fasten off.

FINISHING

Place two pieces WS together and insert the hook into the side of the last row. Working through both pieces, ch 1, then 1 sc in each row and sc around, working sc2tog at the inside corners and 2 sc into each row or sc at the outside corners. When you have joined about two-thirds of the outside edges, stuff some yarn into the cross, then finish joining the two pieces. Join the remaining two pieces in the same way. Use the crochet hook to push all ends inside to hide them. Sew 4 or 5 beads onto the center front of each cross. Attach a jump ring to the top of each cross and close it. Slip another jump ring onto the first one, then slip an ear wire onto the second jump ring and close the jump ring. Repeat for the second earring.

SPARKLY cross earrings

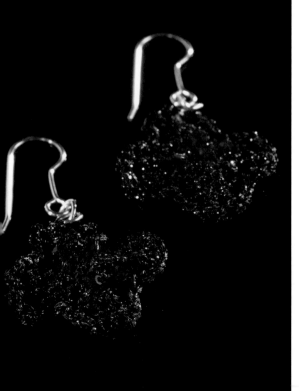

Easy enough for a beginner (as a second or third project perhaps), these little earrings can be made very quickly using leftover yarn and beads. This pair is made in a glittery yarn with sparkling crystal beads—perfect for a party.

Tools and materials
- Hook: steel, size 4 (2mm)
- Yarn: 30yds (27m) fine red Lurex
- Beads: 8–10 red 3mm Swarovski crystal beads
- Findings: 2 ear wires; 4 matching jump rings
- Notions: tapestry needle

Finished size
1" (2.5cm) at widest points

Skill level
Easy

Abbreviations
ch—chain
sc—single crochet
sc2tog—single crochet 2 together (1 stitch decreased)
WS—wrong side

See also
Shaping techniques, pages 32–33
Fastenings and findings, pages 46–47
Sewing on beads and sequins, page 107

These glittery earrings are not only quite easy to make, but also so light that they will be very comfortable to wear. Metallic thread is the perfect choice for special-occasion jewelry; try making the earrings in a range of colors to match different outfits.

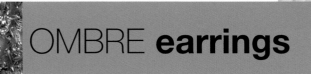

OMBRE **earrings**

MAKING THE EARRINGS (make 2)

Using a beading needle, string 36 beads onto thread.

Row 1: Ch 4 (counts as 1 dc, 1 ch), 4 dc in fourth ch from hook, turn (5 dc).

Rows 2–3: Ch 3, 1 dc in same st as join and in each st across to last st, 2 dc in top of turning ch, turn (9 dc at end of row 3).

Rows 4–5: Ch 3, 1 dc in each st across, turn (9 dc).

Row 6: Sl st in first st, ch 3, pull up 2 beads and chain around them, ch 3, sl st in first st again; sl st in second st, ch 5, pull up 2 beads and chain around them, ch 5, sl st again in second st; repeat in each st across, with chain lengths as follows: 7, 9, 11, 9, 7, 5, 3.
Fasten off.

FINISHING

Sew top of each earring around loop on each ear post. With a tapestry needle, weave in all ends.

Skill level
Easy

Materials
• Hook: size B–1 (2.25mm)
• Thread: 16yds (15m) metallic thread
• Beads: 36 purple size 6° seed beads
• Findings: 2 half-ball sterling silver ear posts with closed loops and 2 ear nuts
• Notions: beading needle; tapestry needle

Finished size
2½" (6.5cm) long x 1½" (4cm) wide

See also
Beaded crochet, page 38
Fastenings and findings, pages 46–47

Abbreviations
ch—chain	sl st—slip stitch
dc—double crochet	st(s)—stitch(es)

MAKING THE EARRINGS (make 2)

Foundation ring: Using A, ch 16 and join with sl st to form a ring.
Round 1: Ch 1, 18 sc in ring, join with sl st in first sc (18 sc).
Break off A and join B.
Round 2: Ch 1, 2 sc in same st as join and in each sc around, join with sl st in first sc (36 sc).
Thread 20 beads onto C.
Break off B and join C.
Round 3: Ch 1, [1 sc, 1 bsc] 10 times, 1 sc, sl st in each of remaining 9 sts, join with sl st in first ch.
Break off C.

FINISHING

With a tapestry needle, weave in all ends. Cut a 16" (41cm) length of wire and fold in half. Insert the crochet hook, front to back, through center sl st of round 3 and pull the wire loop through. Place the free ends of wire through the loop and pull tight. Slip the ear wire loop onto the wire. Wrap wire around itself 4–5 times. Insert crochet hook, front to back, through same center sl st of round 3 and pull the wire through. Wrap the wire around itself to secure. Break off the wire and secure ends neatly.

Tools and materials
- Hook: size B–1 (2.25mm)
- Yarn: 3¼yds (3m) each of blue (A), lilac (B), and purple (C) DK-weight cotton
- Beads: 20 blue 3mm glass beads
- Findings: 2 silver ear wires; 32" (81cm) beading wire
- Notions: tapestry needle

Dangle EARRINGS

Skill level
Easy

These easy-to-make circle earrings could be worked in brightly contrasting colors as well as the toning shades shown here—these would look particularly good with jeans. You could also attach some circles to a cord made from a length of chain to make a matching necklace and bracelet.

Finished size
2" (5cm) diameter

Abbreviations
bsc—beaded single crochet
ch—chain
sc—single crochet
sl st—slip stitch
st(s)—stitch(es)
[ ]—work step in brackets number of times indicated

See also
Beaded crochet, page 38
Fastenings and findings, pages 46–47

These earrings match the choker on pages 60–61 to make a stunning jewelry set that everyone will admire. They can be completed from the leftover materials from the choker. Feel free to vary the number of beads for longer or shorter earrings.

SURFACE crochet earrings

MAKING THE EARRINGS (make 2)

Randomly thread about 22–24 each of size 11° and size 8° seed beads onto the wire.

Foundation chain: 10 bch, bringing up 2 or 3 beads for each chain stitch.

Row 1: With WS facing you, sl st into the top loop of each ch st, bringing up 3 beads for each sl st. These top loops sit just above each bead and you may have to manipulate your hook a little to gain access to them.

Twist tail of wire around the working wire a few times to secure, then with WS still facing you, work a row of beaded surface crochet along the center of the earring, bringing up 2 or 3 beads for each sl st as before, and inserting the hook where it wants to go rather than finding a precise space for each stitch.

Fasten off, leaving a 3" (7.5cm) tail.

FINISHING

Weave the end of the wire through as many beads as possible to secure. Cut wire close to final bead. Attach a jump ring under a couple of loops of wire at the top of each earring. Slip on an ear wire and then close the jump ring.

Skill level
Easy

Materials
- Hook: size B–1 (2.25mm)
- Wire: 2yds (2m) 32-gauge (0.2mm) colored wire
- Beads: ¼oz (6g) mix of size 11° and size 8° seed beads
- Findings: 2 gold jump rings; 2 gold ear wires
- Notions: beading needle

Finished size
1¾" (4.5cm) long

See also
Surface crochet, page 36
Beaded crochet, page 38
Wire crochet, page 39
Fastenings and findings, pages 46–47

Abbreviations
bch—beaded chain	sl st—slip stitch
ch—chain	WS—wrong side

MAKING THE EARRINGS (make 2)

Note: Beginning with round 2, make the first st of each round in the same st as the join. Thread 37 seed beads onto the wire.

Foundation chain: 15 bch, ch 1 (16 ch total). To work first round, turn chain so beads are facing you (back of chain); this is the bottom of the earring.

Round 1: Working into top of chain only, 1 sc in second ch from hook and in each ch across, ending with 3 sc in last ch. Continuing up other side of ch, 1 sc in next ch and in each ch across, ending with 2 sc in first ch, join with sl st in first ch (32 sc).

Round 2: Ch 1, [1 sc, sc2tog] 5 times, 3 so in next st, [sc2tog, 1 sc] 5 times, 3 sc in last st, join with sl st in first st (26 sts).

Round 3: Ch 1, [sc2tog, 1 sc] 3 times, sc2tog, 3 sc in next st, [sc2tog, sc] 4 times, 3 sc in next st, 1 sc in next st, join with sl st in first st (22 sts).

Round 4: Ch 1, turn, 1 bsc in first st and in each st around, join with sl st in first st (22 sts). Fasten off.

Tools and materials
- Hook: steel, size 8 (1.5mm)
- Wire: 15yds (14m) 28-gauge (0.3mm) silver wire
- Beads: 37 opalescent gold size 8° seed beads; 2 pale yellow 6mm glass drop beads; 2 metallic gold 2mm round beads
- Findings: 2 silver head pins; 4 silver eye pins; 2 silver ear wires; 2 silver 3mm jump rings
- Notions: round-nose pliers; wire cutters

Chandelier DROP EARRINGS

Skill level
Advanced

FINISHING
For each earring, secure all wire ends. Using the photo as a guide, attach an eye pin to each tip of the earring, making a loop at the other end of the pin so that it measures about ½" (13mm) long. Join the loops of the eye pins with a jump ring. Attach an ear wire to the jump ring. Thread a drop bead and gold bead onto a head pin. Trim the head pin and make a loop at the end. Secure this around the middle of cast-on chain row.

Use wire and beads to create these classic earrings with a timeless silhouette. Although the techniques used to make them are not difficult, crocheting with fine wire requires a degree of skill past intermediate.

Finished size
1¼" (3cm) at widest; 1" (2.5cm) long excluding drop bead and hanging wires

Abbreviations
bch—beaded chain
bsc—beaded single crochet
ch—chain
sc—single crochet
sc2tog—single crochet 2 together (1 stitch decreased)
sl st—slip stitch
st(s)—stitch(es)
[ ]—work step in brackets number of times indicated

See also
Beaded crochet, page 38
Wire crochet, page 39
Fastenings and findings, pages 46–47

CHAPTER 5

Pins

Pins are an easy way to dress up an outfit, and can be

pinned onto accessories and garments alike. Choose from

floral and rosette designs to feather and butterfly pins. As well

as using yarn, there are pins made from hemp and raffia—

never be afraid to experiment with materials.

FRILLY **flower pins**

The pattern gives instructions for making the pink frilly flower; the green flower is an example of the frillier variation and is made using ribbon yarn without any beaded embellishment. For a smaller flower, simply use a finer yarn.

MAKING THE PINS

Foundation ring: Using A and B held together, ch 4 and join with sl st to form a ring.

Round 1: Ch 3 (counts as 1 dc), 10 dc in ring, join with sl st in top of beg ch-3 (11 dc).

Round 2: Ch 1, 2 sc in each dc around, join with sl st in first sc (22 sc).

Round 3: Ch 3, 3 dc in same st as join, 4 dc in each sc around, join with sl st in top of beg ch-3 (88 dc).

Cut A, leaving a 3" (7.5cm) tail for weaving in. Continue using B only.

Round 4: Ch 1, 2 sc in each dc around, join with sl st in first sc (176 sc).

Fasten off.

Variation: For a frillier version, work 3 sc in every stitch on round 4 instead of 2.

CENTER EMBELLISHMENT

Using a beading needle, join beading thread to outside edge of any dc on round 1. Pick up one sequin and one size 11° seed bead, then skip the seed bead and go back through the sequin only and into the flower. Repeat around the outside edge of center, placing the sequins evenly.

Move to just inside the ring of sequins, pick up one size 8° bead and one size 11° bead, skip the smaller bead, and take needle back through the larger bead and into the flower. Repeat until inner circle is filled with beads.

FINISHING

With a tapestry needle, weave in all ends. Sew a pin back to the back of the flower about 1¼" (3cm) below the outer edge.

Tools and materials
- Hook: size H–8 (5mm)
- Yarn: 45yds (41m) novelty yarn (A); small amount of contrasting metallic thread (B)
- Beads/sequins: 9 pink 5mm sequins; 16 clear and/or frosted purple size 8° seed beads, 25 pink size 11° seed beads
- Findings: 1¼–1½" (3–4cm) long pin back (1 per flower)
- Notions: beading needle; beading thread; tapestry needle

Finished size
3½" (9cm) diameter

Abbreviations
beg—begin(ning)
ch—chain
dc—double crochet
sc—single crochet
sl st—slip stitch

REMINDER: SEWING ON BEADS AND SEQUINS

1 Join the thread with a few small, neat stitches. Pick up a sequin and a small seed bead with the needle.

2 Skipping the seed bead, take the needle back through the sequin and into the flower.

3 Pick up a large and then a small seed bead on the needle.

4 Skip the small bead and take the needle back through the large bead and into the flower.

5 If you want to sew a single sequin or bead in place, simply take the needle through the sequin or bead and into the crochet.

This dramatic pin will look great on a big sweater or to make a statement on a winter coat. You could even use it to accessorize a hat. It is such a lovely shape that you may wish to make several in different color combinations.

FLUTTERBY **pin**

Skill level
Intermediate

Tools and materials

- Hook: steel, size 4 (2mm)
- Yarn: 90yds (82m) red DK-weight cotton
- Embroidery: scraps of purple, turquoise, and gray embroidery thread; flexible green beading wire
- Beads: 8 frosted gold 4mm round beads; 20 green 7mm bugle beads; 3 different-colored 10–15mm glass beads for body
- Findings: 3¼" (8cm) long silver hat pin
- Notions: tapestry needle

Finished size

5½" (14cm) at widest x
4½" (11.5cm) at longest

Abbreviations

ch—chain
sc—single crochet
sl st—slip stitch

See also

Sewing on beads and sequins, page 107

Note

For each row, you will not be at the end when you turn.

MAKING THE PIN

SMALL WING (make 2)

Foundation chain: Ch 13.

Row 1: 1 sc in second ch from hook and in each of next 10 ch, 3 sc in last ch. Continuing up other side of ch, 1 sc in each next 9 ch, turn.

Rows 2–4: Ch 1, skip first sc, 1 sc in each of next 9 sc, 3 sc in end sc, 1 sc in each of next 9 sc along other side, turn (five peaks around wing).

Row 5: Ch 1, skip first sc, 1 sc in each of next 9 sc, 3 sc in end sc, sl st in next sc.
Fasten off.

LARGE WING (make 2)

Foundation chain: Ch 17.

Row 1: 1 sc in second ch from hook and in each of next 14 ch, 3 sc in last ch. Continuing up other side of ch, 1 sc in each of next 12 ch, turn.

Rows 2–8: Ch 1, skip first sc, 1 sc in each of next 12 sc, 3 sc in end sc, 1 sc in each of next 12 sc along other side, turn.

Row 9: Ch 1, skip first sc, 1 sc in each next 12 sc, sl st in remaining sc.
Fasten off.

FINISHING

With a tapestry needle, weave in all ends. Using the photo as a guide, stitch the two large wings together, then repeat with the small wings. With the smaller pair on top, stitch the two pairs of wings together. Sew four gold beads down the center of each small wing, following the central line of crochet; sew a curved V-shape of 10 bugle beads onto the large wings, following the lines of crochet. Decorate the large wings with embroidery, starting with a small circle of purple chain stitch. Surround this with rings of backstitch in turquoise, green wire, and gray. Sew the body beads down the center of the butterfly, then insert the hat pin through them.

REMINDER: CHAIN STITCH AND BACKSTITCH EMBROIDERY

1 To work chain stitch, bring the needle to the front of the crochet, *then take it to the back at the same place, leaving a loop at the front.

2 Bring the needle to the front again just inside the end of the loop. Repeat from * to work each chain stitch.

3 Secure the loop of the final chain stitch with a small stitch over the end of the loop, then secure the ends of the thread.

4 Work the first ring of backstitch around the chain stitch circle.

5 Add another two rings of backstitch to complete the wing decoration.

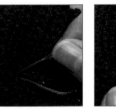

FLUFFY **rosette pin**

Wear this pin on a hat, jacket, coat, blouse, or even a purse. You can change the look of the pin with your choice of yarn. Synthetic yarn, such as nylon, will make a very delicate piece suitable for a dressy outfit, whereas this mohair version is a fun pin to put on a winter hat or coat. You can also experiment with the many different novelty yarns that are widely available.

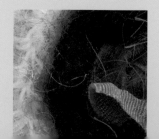

MAKING THE PIN

SMALL ROSETTE

Foundation ring: Using A, ch 4 and join with sl st to form a ring.

Round 1: Ch 1, 7 sc in ring, join with sl st in first sc.

Round 2: Ch 3 (counts as 1 dc), 1 dc in same st as join, *2 dc in next sc; repeat from * around, join with sl st in top of beg ch-3 (14 dc).

Round 3: Ch 3, 2 dc in next dc, *1 dc in next dc, 2 dc in next dc; repeat from * around, join with sl st in top of beg ch-3 (21 dc).
Fasten off.

MEDIUM ROSETTE

Foundation ring: Using B, ch 4 and join with sl st to form a ring.

Round 1: Ch 3 (counts as 1 dc), 6 dc in ring, join with sl st in top of beg ch-3 (7 dc).

Rounds 2–3: Work as for small rosette, but do not fasten off at end of round 3.

Round 4: Ch 3, 1 dc in next dc, *2 dc in next dc, 1 dc in each of next 2 dc; repeat from * to last st, 2 dc in last st, join with sl st in top of beg ch-3 (28 dc).

Round 5: Ch 3, *3 dc in next dc, 1 dc in next dc, 1 sc in next dc, 1 dc in next dc; repeat from * to last 3 sts, 3 dc in next dc, 1 dc in next dc, 1 sc in next dc, join with sl st in top of beg ch-3 (42 sts).
Fasten off.

LARGE ROSETTE

Using yarn C, work as for medium rosette through round 4.

Round 5: Ch 3, 1 dc in next dc, *2 dc in next dc, 1 dc in each of next 2 dc; repeat from * to last 2 sts, 2 dc in next st, 1 dc in last st, join with sl st in top of beg ch-3 (37 dc).

Round 6: Ch 3, *1 dc in each of next 3 dc, 2 dc in next dc, 1 dc in each of next 4 dc, 2 dc in next dc; repeat from * across, join with sl st in top of beg ch-3 (45 dc).
Fasten off.

FRILLY OUTER ROSETTE

Using C, work as for large rosette through round 6 (45 dc); do not fasten off.

Round 7: Work round 4 of medium rosette (60 dc).

Round 8: Ch 1, *1 hdc in next dc, 1 dc in next dc, 3 dc in next dc, 1 dc in next dc, 1 hdc in next dc; repeat from * around, join with sl st in top of first hdc.
Fasten off.

FINISHING

With a tapestry needle, weave in all ends. Layer the four rosettes slightly off-center and sew together in the middle with the ribbon. Sew a pin back to the back of the rosette.

Tools and materials
- Hook: steel, size 8 (1.5mm)
- Yarn: 11yds (10m) red (A), 20yds (18m) blue (B), and 50yds (46m) green (C) laceweight mohair
- Findings: 1½" (4cm) long pin back
- Notions: tapestry needle; sewing needle; short length of green ribbon

Finished size
3½" (9cm) diameter

Abbreviations
beg—begin(ning)
ch—chain
dc—double crochet
hdc—half double crochet
sc—single crochet
sl st—slip stitch
st(s)—stitch(es)

See also
Fastenings and findings, pages 46–47

REMINDER: SHAPING THE FRILLY EDGE OF THE OUTER ROSETTE

 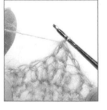 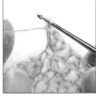 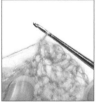 

1 Each frill in round 8 starts with 1 hdc, which has a shorter stitch length than the dc stitches.

2 Work 1 dc after the hdc to extend the frill outward by increasing the stitch length.

3 Form the fullest part of the frill by working 3 dc into the next stitch.

4 Work 1 dc in the following stitch.

5 Finish each frill with 1 hdc, pulling the frilly edge inward once more.

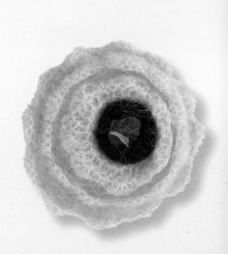

This flower pin borrows a technique from traditional Irish crochet and brings it into the high-fashion realm with the use of torn raffia and beads. You could try making it using all sorts of different materials, from novelty yarn to garden twine.

Abbreviations

ch—chain
dc—double crochet
dc2tog—double crochet 2 together (1 stitch decreased)
fpsc—front post single crochet

sc—single crochet
sl st—slip stitch
sp(s)—space(s)
WS—wrong side
[ ]—work step in brackets number of times indicated

RAFFIA flower pin

MAKING THE PIN

Foundation ring: Ch 5 and join with sl st to form a ring.

Round 1: Ch 1, [1 sc in ring, ch 2, dc2tog in ring, ch 2] 6 times, join with sl st in first sc (6 sc, 6 dc).

Round 2: Ch 1, 1 sc in first sc, [ch 4, 1 sc in next sc, skipping ch-2 sp, dc, and ch-2 sp] 5 times, ch 4, join with sl st in first sc (6 sc, 6 ch-2 sps).

Round 3: [Ch 2, 6 dc in ch-4 sp, ch 2, sl st in next sc] 6 times, turn.

Round 4 (WS): Ch 1, 1 fpsc around first sc of round 2, [ch 6, 1 fpsc around next sc of round 2] 5 times, ch 6, join with sl st in first fpsc, turn.

Round 5: [Ch 2, 9 dc in ch-6 sp, ch 2, sl st in next fpsc] 6 times.

Round 6 (WS): Ch 1, 1 fpsc around first fpsc of round 4, [ch 8, 1 fpsc around next fpsc of round 4] 5 times, ch 8, join with sl st in first fpsc, turn.

Round 7: [Ch 2, 11 dc in ch-8 sp, ch 2, sl st in next fpsc] 6 times.
Fasten off.

FINISHING

With a tapestry needle, weave in all ends. Sew 3 beads onto the center front of the flower, then sew a pin back onto WS.

Skill level
Intermediate

Tools and materials
- Hook: size G–6 (4mm)
- Raffia: ½oz (14g) purple raffia; tear lengths of raffia into 2–3 thinner strips and knot the ends of each strip together to make a continuous thread that is easier to crochet with than thicker strands of raffia
- Beads: 3 green 5mm wooden beads
- Findings: 1¼" (3cm) long pin back
- Notions: tapestry needle

Finished size
3½" (9cm) diameter

See also
Raised stitches, page 34
Fastenings and findings, pages 46–47
Sewing on beads and sequins, page 107

MAKING THE PIN

LARGE FEATHER (make 1)
Foundation chain: Ch 41.
Row 1: Sl st in second ch from hook and in each of next 4 ch. Working 1 st in each ch, work 8 sc, 8 hdc, 8 dc, 10 tr, ending with 5 tr in last ch. Continuing up other side of ch, working 1 st in each ch, work 8 tr, 6 dc, 6 hdc, 9 sc, 1 sl st.
Fasten off.

MEDIUM FEATHER (make 2)
Foundation chain: Ch 31.
Row 1: Sl st in second ch from hook and in each of next 4 ch. Working 1 st into each ch, work 5 sc, 5 hdc, 5 dc, 9 tr, ending with 5 tr in last ch. Continuing up other side of ch, working 1 st in each ch, work 9 tr, 5 dc, 7 sc, 3 sl st.
Fasten off.

SMALL FEATHER (make 4)
Foundation chain: Ch 27.
Row 1: Sl st in second ch from hook and in each of next 2 ch. Working 1 st in each ch, work 2 sl st, 4 sc, 4 hdc, 5 dc, 9 tr, ending with 5 tr in last ch. Continuing up other side of ch, working 1 st in each ch, work 9 tr, 5 dc, 7 sc, 3 sl st.
Fasten off.

Tools and materials
- Hook: steel, size 4 (2mm)
- Yarn: 60yds (55m) cream sportweight wool (A); 60yds (55m) cream superfine mohair (B); use A and B held together throughout
- Sequins/beads: 40–45 gold 6mm cup sequins; 40–45 bronze 2mm beads
- Findings: 1" (2.5cm) long pin back
- Notions: tapestry needle

Fancy FEATHER PIN

Skill level
Intermediate

FINISHING
With a tapestry needle, weave in all ends. Stitch the feathers together, using the photo as a guide. Start with the four small feathers pointing outward, then the two medium feathers, and finish with the large central feather. Overlap the base of the feathers, with the small feathers outermost and the large feather innermost. Felt the finished feather. When dry, sew a sequin topped with a bead onto the front of the pin in a pleasing arrangement. Turn the pin over and sew a pin back in place.

This wool and mohair pin is delightfully soft and fluffy. Wear it as a bold fastening on a cozy wrap, or to adorn a plain outfit. For a jazzy look, work the individual feathers in different colors.

Finished size
7½" (19cm) long x 5" (12.5cm) wide after felting

Abbreviations
ch—chain
dc—double crochet
hdc—half double crochet
sc—single crochet
sl st—slip stitch
tr—treble crochet

See also
Fastenings and findings, pages 46–47
Sewing on beads and sequins, page 107
Felting, page 118

Note
For each row, you will not be at the end when you fasten off.

HEMP **disk pins**

Skill level
Easy

These pins can be made from any number of things you can find around your home: packing cord, raffia, paper string, or garden twine. All of these materials can be either dyed or used in their natural state. However, don't forget to explore your stash of leftover balls of yarn, and if you come across any beads that look as if they will complement the working material, you could add them to round 3 of the inner disks.

MAKING THE PINS

TWO-DISK PIN
Outer disk
Foundation ring: Using A, ch 20 and join with sl st to form a ring.
Round 1: Ch 1 (counts as 1 sc), 29 sc in ring, join with sl st in first ch (30 sc).
Round 2: Ch 1, 1 sc in each st around, join with sl st in first ch.
Round 3: Ch 3 (counts as 1 dc), 1 dc in same st as join tbl, 2 dc tbl in each st around, join with sl st in top of beg ch-3 (60 dc).
Round 4: *Ch 4, sl st in second ch from hook, ch 1, skip 1 dc, sl st in next dc; repeat from * around (30 picots).
Fasten off.

Inner disk
Work as for outer disk through round 2.
Round 3: Ch 1, *1 sc in center of ring; repeat from * around, arranging long yarn threads neatly on RS, working until disk is covered.
Fasten off.

THREE-DISK PIN
Outer disk
Using B, work as for outer disk of the two-disk pin through round 3.
Round 4: Ch 1, *insert hook through front loop of first st of round 2 and in center of ring, yo, draw through first loop on hook, yo and draw through remaining 2 loops, 1 sc in next st from round 3; repeat from * around, join with sl st to first ch (30 long sc, 30 short sc).
Round 5: *Ch 4, sl st in second ch from hook, ch 2, sl st in the next short sc of round 4; repeat from * around (30 picots).
Fasten off.

Inner disk
Using cord A, work as for inner disk of the two-disk pin.

Center disk
Foundation ring: Using C, ch 10 and join with sl st to form a ring.
Round 1: Ch 1 (counts as 1 sc), 14 sc in ring, join with sl st in first ch (15 sc).
Round 2: Ch 1, 1 sc in each st around, join with sl st in first ch (15 sc).
Round 3: Work as for round 3 of inner disk.
Fasten off.

FINISHING
With a tapestry needle, weave in all ends and finish each disk by threading the ends under both top loops of the first stitch of the last round and back through the center of the last stitch worked. Weave in on the reverse side to secure. Starting with the outer disks and working inward, attach each disk to the next one with whipstitch. Using an old pair of scissors and protective eye and hand covers, cut the pin fixture bar near both ends, leaving enough at each end to sew to pin. Turn the cut pieces outward and sew them to the back of the pin on either side of the central hole.

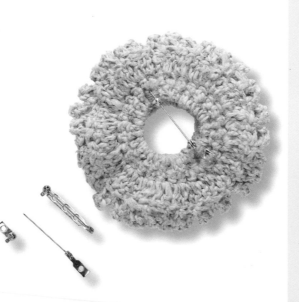

Tools and materials
- Hook: size C–2 (2.75mm)
- Yarn/string: both styles—hemp beading cord (A); three-disk pin only—sportweight cotton yarn (B) and metallic Lurex yarn (C); outer disks require 17yds (15.5m) each, inner disks 6½yds (6m) each, center disk 4yds (3.5m)
- Findings: pin back (1 per pin)
- Notions: tapestry needle; old pair of scissors and protective eye and hand covers; sewing thread and needle

Finished size
Two-disk pin = 4" (10cm) diameter
Three-disk pin = 3¼" (8cm) diameter

Abbreviations
beg—begin(ning)
ch—chain
dc—double crochet
RS—right side
sc—single crochet
sl st—slip stitch
st(s)—stitch(es)
tbl—through back loop
yo—yarn over

See also
Fastenings and findings, pages 46–47

Note
If the hemp cord looks smooth, then it has probably been sized. Size is a glue-type substance that can usually be soaked off by immersing the cord in warm water for an hour or two. The hemp cord used in the three-disk pin has been soaked, making it less stiff and easier to work; it also gives the pin a slightly hairy texture.

CHAPTER 6

Rings

While it may surprise many people, rings are very easy to make using basic crochet techniques. The spotty and flower rings only require the smallest scraps of yarn, a ring shank, and buttons, or you can make a classic beaded ring using wire or thread and a selection of your favorite beads.

SPOTTY **rings**

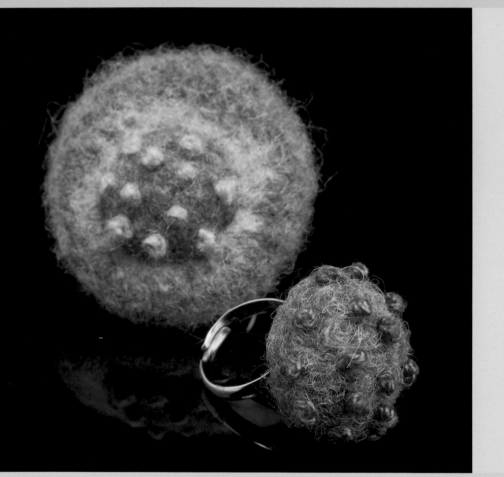

Felting might disguise the individual crochet stitches but not the style in these simply made and embroidered spotty rings. You could easily adapt the stuffed balls into earrings, or use the large spotty disk as a necklace pendant.

Felting

This is a process of shrinking a woolen fabric by washing it in soapy water to bind the fibers together to create a more solid and fluffy fabric. Felting will not work with superwash wools, cottons, or synthetic yarns. It can be done by hand but is easier in a washing machine. Place the pieces to be felted in a mesh lingerie bag. Place in the washing machine with about 1 tablespoon of detergent and several other items to be washed. (Having other items in the wash will speed up the felting process because it will cause more agitation. Be sure the items will not shed fibers, or the shed fibers will get felted into your piece.) Set the washer on smallest load and hot water, and start. Check the progress about every 10 minutes at first, then more frequently as the felting begins, resetting the machine as needed to continue the agitation. When the piece is felted to desired size, rinse by hand in warm water. Remove excess water either by using the spin cycle on the machine, or by rolling the piece in a towel and squeezing. Ease the damp piece into shape by pulling, patting, and smoothing as necessary. Allow to air-dry. Felting is very much a case of trial and error, because the water temperature and agitation strength of each washing machine varies. It is therefore a good idea to felt a test swatch first.

MAKING THE RINGS

SMALL SPOTTY RING

Foundation ring: Using A, ch 4 and join with sl st to form a ring.

Round 1: Ch 1, 8 sc in ring, join with sl st in first ch (8 sc).

Round 2: Ch 1, 2 sc in each sc around, join with sl st in first ch (16 sc).

Rounds 3–5: Ch 1, 1 sc in each sc around, join with sl st in first ch.

Round 6: Ch 1, sc2tog around, join with sl st in first ch (8 sc).
Fasten off.

FINISHING

Cut some short lengths of yarn to use as stuffing. Insert the stuffing into the crocheted ball, then sew the ball closed using a tapestry needle and yarn. Weave in all ends, then felt the ball. When dry, decorate with French knots using pink embroidery thread. Glue the bottom of the ball onto the ring shank; tie a piece of scrap yarn around it to hold the pieces firmly together while the glue dries.

LARGE SPOTTY RING

Using B, work the center ball as for the small spotty ring (up to felting).
Make outer circle as follows.

Foundation ring: Using C, ch 16 and join with sl st to form a ring.

Round 1: Ch 1, 20 sc in ring, join with sl st in first ch (20 sc).
Break off C and join D.

Round 2: Using D, ch 1, 1 sc in each of next 5 sc, 1 hdc in each of next 4 sc, 2 dc in each of next 3 sc, 1 hdc in each of next 4 sc, 1 sc in each of next 4 sc, join with sl st in first ch (23 sts).
Fasten off.

FINISHING

With a tapestry needle, weave in all ends. Felt both pieces. Sew the stuffed ball to the center of the outer circle. Decorate the ball with French knots using mint green embroidery thread. Complete as for the small spotty ring.

Tools and materials
- Hook: steel, size 4 (2mm)
- Yarn: 3¼yds (3m) each of lilac (A), grass green (B), mint green (C), and turquoise (D) sportweight wool
- Thread: scraps of pink and mint green embroidery thread
- Findings: 2 silver ring shanks
- Notions: tapestry needle; superglue

Finished size
Small = ¾–1" (2–2.5cm) diameter
Large = 2" (5cm) diameter

Abbreviations
ch—chain
dc—double crochet
hdc—half double crochet
sc—single crochet
sc2tog—single crochet 2 together (1 stitch decreased)
sl st—slip stitch
st(s)—stitch(es)

REMINDER: FRENCH KNOT EMBROIDERY AND ATTACHING A RING SHANK

1 Secure the embroidery thread at the back of the ring, then bring the needle through to the required position for the first French knot.

2 Wrap the thread twice around the needle. Pulling the thread taut, take the needle through the crochet to the next French knot position.

3 Continue making French knots in this way, scattering them fairly evenly over the ring.

4 Apply some glue to the bottom of the crocheted piece, then press firmly onto the ring shank.

5 Tie some spare yarn around the crocheted piece and the shank until the glue dries and they are firmly stuck together.

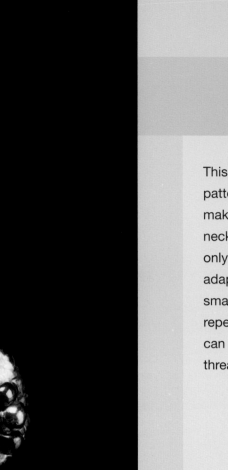

This is more a technique than a pattern, and can be adapted to make any number of bracelets, necklaces, or even earrings. The only thing to remember when adapting these ideas is that using small beads or small pattern repeats will mean that the sizing can be more accurate. Strong thread and good light is essential.

BEADED rings

MAKING THE RINGS

FLOWER MOTIF RING

Use white thread and leave a 2ft (61cm) tail of thread.

St 1: Pb (3 green beads) onto the hook, yo, draw loop through beads.

St 2: Pb (1 green, 1 red, 1 green bead) onto the hook, yo, draw loop through beads and loop on the hook.

St 3: Pb (1 red, 1 gold, 1 red bead) onto the hook, yo, draw loop through beads and loop on the hook.

St 4: Repeat st 2.

Repeat these 4 sts nine more times or until the beaded length fits comfortably around the finger knuckle.

Work the edges as follows.

Bring the ends together. Insert the hook through the beads on st 1, yo, draw the thread through the beads and the last loop as if to fasten off.

Now working into the loops formed on the top of each column of beads, insert the hook into second st, yo, draw a loop through, ch 1.

Row 1: *1 sc in next st, ch 1; repeat from * across.

Fasten off.

Working along the bottom of the beaded sts using the tail, insert the hook into last st, yo, draw a loop through, ch 1.

Repeat row 1.

Fasten off.

FINISHING

With a tapestry needle, weave in all ends.

Tools and materials

- Hook: steel, size 14 (0.75mm)
- Thread: 4ft (1.2m) white or black size 40 crochet cotton for each ring
- Beads (adjust quantities if necessary to suit size of ring):

  Flower motif ring—70 green, 40 red, and 10 gold 2mm round glass beads

  Central stone ring—66 silver metal 2mm round beads; 2 light blue 10mm bugle beads; 2 frosted white 3mm cube beads; 1 blue/green 6mm round glass focal bead

  Bugle bead ring—9 blue/purple 10mm bugle beads; 18 red 2mm round glass beads; 9 light blue 3mm cube beads

  Silver crimp ring—30 silver 2mm crimps
- Notions: tapestry needle

Finished size

2¾" (7cm) circumference; adjust the number of stitches worked to fit your finger

Abbreviations

ch—chain
pb—place bead(s)
sc—single crochet
st(s)—stitch(es)
yo—yarn over

REMINDER: PLACING BEADS AND WORKING THE EDGE

1 Place the first set of beads onto the hook, wrap the yarn over the hook, then draw a loop of yarn through the beads.

2 Place the second set of beads onto the hook, yo, then draw the yarn through the beads and the loop on the hook.

3 Repeat this process to add each subsequent set of beads until the ring fits around the finger knuckle.

4 Join the ends by inserting the hook through the first set of beads, yo, then draw yarn through the beads and last loop on the hook.

5 Work 1 sc, ch 1 around each edge of the ring to neaten the edges and frame the beads attractively.

SILVER CRIMP RING

Use the same beaded crochet technique as for the flower motif ring, but with just 1 silver crimp on each stitch. Work 30 stitches. Finish as for the flower motif ring, but work a row of sc around the edges instead.

BUGLE BEAD RING

Use the same beaded crochet technique as for the flower motif ring, but with black thread and the following beads.

St 1: 1 blue bugle bead.
St 2: 1 red bead, 1 blue cube bead, 1 red bead.
Repeat these two stitches eight more times.
Finish as for the flower motif ring.

CENTRAL STONE RING

Use the same beaded crochet technique as for the flower motif ring, but with the following beads.

Sts 1–10: 3 silver beads on each st.
St 11: 1 silver bead, 1 cube bead, 1 silver bead.
St 12: 1 blue bugle bead.
St 13: 1 silver bead, 1 focal bead, 1 silver bead.
St 14: 1 blue bugle bead.
St 15: 1 silver bead, 1 cube bead, 1 silver bead.
Sts 16–25: 3 silver beads on each st.
Finish as for the flower motif ring.

This ring is a snap to work up, and no one will believe that you made it using hairpin crochet. It is worth investing in some really special accent beads to form a fitting focal point on this beautiful ring.

HAIRPIN **wire ring**

MAKING THE RING

For each strip, thread the beads onto the wire in the following sequence: [A, 64 C, B, 64 C] twice, A, 32 C.

Work strip (make 2): Set loom to 2½" (6.5cm). Catch an A or B bead in every other stitch of the hairpin strip; they will align on one side (RS) of the strip only. Catch 32 C beads in each loop. Use a twisted loop on the starting pin instead of a slipknot, taking care that the first 32 C beads are caught in this first loop. Catch the A bead, starting in the first stitch. Work 10 loops in total. Fasten off. Leave 6" (15cm) tails at end.

Form ring: Bend the tips of the loops toward each other and join them with a 1x1 cable join, starting from the beginning of the strip and keeping the RS facing out. Make sure when joining that the beads are evenly divided between each leg of the loop. Thread 16 C onto tail, bring through last loop of cable join to secure, thread another 16 C onto tail, and secure end to spine of strip; make sure to keep the tail the same length as the other strips.

FINISHING

Secure and trim all wire ends. Try on the ring. Pinch the spine under the focal beads to adjust the ring for a perfect fit.

Skill level
Advanced

Tools and materials
- Hook: steel, size 7 (1.65mm)
- Hairpin loom
- Wire: 5yds (4.5m) 28-gauge (0.3mm) gold wire
- Beads: 3 clear 10mm handblown glass beads (A); 2 bronze 7mm pearls (B); 192 gold 2mm seed beads (C)

Finished size
¾" (2cm) diameter

See also
Hairpin crochet, pages 40–41
Cable techniques, page 42

Abbreviations
RS—right side
[ ]—work step in brackets number of times indicated

These rings are super easy. If you are a complete beginner, try the yellow, then blue, then pink ring. Choose bright primary colors for the best results.

FUNKY **flower rings**

MAKING THE RINGS

YELLOW RING
Foundation ring: Using A, ch 4 and join with sl st to form a ring.
Round 1: Ch 1, [1 sc in ring, ch 8] 12 times, join with sl st in first sc (12 ch-8 lps).
Round 2: Ch 1, 1 sc in same st as join, ch 12, [1 sc in next sc, ch 12] 11 times, join with sl st in first sc (12 ch-12 lps).
Fasten off.

BLUE RING
Foundation ring: Using B, ch 4 and join with sl st to form a ring.
Round 1: Ch 1, 8 sc in ring, join with sl st in first sc. Work first petal as follows.
Row 1 (RS): Ch 1, 1 sc in each of next 2 sc, turn.
Row 2 (WS): Ch 1, [2 sc in next sc] twice, turn (4 sc).
Row 3: Ch 1, [2 sc in next sc] 4 times, turn (8 sc).
Row 4: Ch 1, 1 sc in each sc across, turn.
Row 5: Ch 1, sc2tog, 1 sc in each of next 4 sc, sc2tog (6 sc).
Fasten off.
Work three more petals in the same way as the first, joining yarn into next sc of round 1 after previous petal.
When you have finished row 5 of the fourth petal, ch 1 instead of fastening off.
Continue by working 1 sc in each row and sc around petal, working sc2tog at the first row of each petal (between petals) and 2 sc in both corner sts of row 5.
Fasten off.

PINK RING
Foundation ring: Using C, ch 4 and join with sl st to form a ring.
Round 1 (RS): Ch 1, 1 sc in ring, [ch 4, 1 sc in ring] 5 times, ch 4, join with sl st in first sc (6 ch-4 sps).
Round 2: Ch 1, work (1 sc, 1 hdc, 2 dc, 1 hdc, 1 sc) in each ch-4 sp, join with sl st in first sc, turn.
Round 3 (WS): Ch 1, 1 fpsc around first sc of round 1, [ch 5, 1 fpsc around next sc of round 1] 5 times, ch 5, join with sl st in first fpsc, turn (6 ch-5 sps).
Round 4 (RS): Ch 1, work (1 sc, 1 hdc, 3 dc, 1 hdc, 1 sc) in each ch-5 sp, join with sl st in first sc.
Fasten off.

FINISHING
With a tapestry needle, weave in all ends. Sew the beads onto the center of each flower (onto WS for yellow ring and RS for blue and pink rings). Sew each flower onto its corresponding button. Glue the flat side of the button onto the ring shank, holding the pieces together tightly for a few seconds until they bond, then allow to dry completely.

THE **designers**

This book is a collaborative work, and features crochet jewelry projects from an international cast of designers to provide a wide range of jewelry styles.

Jenny Dowde
www.jennydowde.com
jdesigns@tpg.com.au

Jenny began her textile art career as a knitwear designer in early 1990. Since 1997 she has been working in and teaching the medium of free-form knitting and crochet using fiber as well as wire and beads. Jenny is the author of three books and her work has been featured in various international magazines. She lives in Wollongong in New South Wales, Australia. Jenny's projects are:

- *Barrel bead necklace, pages 52–53*
- *Amulet purse, pages 58–59*
- *Surface crochet choker, pages 60–61*
- *Shell necklace, page 62*
- *Beaded chain bracelet, page 79*
- *Frilly floral bangles, pages 80–81*
- *Surface crochet earrings, page 102*
- *Frilly flower pins, pages 106–107*

Jennifer Hansen
www.stitchdiva.com

Jennifer Hansen lives in Fremont, California, where she is a full-time crochet and knit designer, teacher, and writer. Her innovative crochet work has been featured in various books, magazines, and television shows, and she also publishes designs through her company, Stitch Diva Studios. Stitch Diva Studios patterns are available for download, and may also be purchased at yarn stores nationwide. Jennifer is passionate about the craft, and wants to contribute to the joy that everyone can find in creating beautiful things. Her professional background is in architecture and information technology. Jennifer's projects are:

- *Hairpin bead necklace, pages 66–67*
- *Hairpin wire bangle, pages 86–87*
- *Hoop earrings, page 94*
- *Chandelier drop earrings, page 103*
- *Hairpin wire ring, page 123*

Yoko Hatta
www.kazekobo.net
kazekobo@nifty.com

Yoko trained as a designer at art college, then became part of a trend in Japan known as the "Mansion Makers," a fashion design movement in Tokyo during the 1960s and early 1970s where young designers set up their own small brands, supplying boutiques and shops or selling from their own studios. With her company, Kazekobo, Yoko has become one of the most popular and well-established handicraft designers in Japan. In addition to designing, Yoko regularly appears on a television fashion program, gives lectures, teaches, has published several books, and writes articles for magazines. She lives and works in Tokyo. Yoko's projects are:

- *Circle necklace, pages 56–57*
- *Chunky flower bracelet, pages 72–73*
- *Sparkly cross earrings, page 99*
- *Raffia flower pin, page 112*
- *Funky flower rings, pages 124–125*

Waejong Kim & Anna Pulvermakher
www.loopymango.com
117 Front St., Brooklyn, NY 11201

Anna and Waejong met at New York's Fashion Institute of Technology. Their shared passion for crochet led to the foundation of a boutique, Loopy Mango, in New York's vibrant East Village. Less than two years later, Loopy Mango grew almost three times in size and moved to a bigger space across the Manhattan Bridge to one of Brooklyn's up-and-coming neighborhoods called Dumbo (Down Under Manhattan Bridge Overpass). Loopy Mango specializes in handmade clothes and jewelry, latest fashions, and unique vintage pieces. Loopy Mango designs have been featured in several international style magazines. Waejong and Anna's projects are:

- *Big bead necklace, pages 50–51*
- *Multicolor necklace, page 63*
- *Cobweb bracelet, page 85*
- *Snowmen earrings, pages 92–93*
- *Circle earrings, page 95*
- *Fluffy rosette pin, pages 110–111*

Karen Klemp
www.almostamy.com

Karen, former president of the Crochet Guild of America, owns and operates Almost Amy, a fiber arts and jewelry design studio in Arlington, Virginia. She teaches workshops at many regional and national fiber arts conferences as well as locally, in northern Virginia. Karen's website showcases her designs and provides a schedule of the workshops she teaches. Karen's projects are:

- *Hoop choker, page 54*
- *Glasses keeper, page 55*
- *Gemstone lariat, pages 64–65*
- *Shell cuff bracelet, pages 74–75*
- *Ombre earrings, page 100*

Carol Meldrum
www.beatknit.com

Carol graduated with an honors degree in constructed textiles, and now teaches knitting and crochet workshops throughout the United Kingdom. Formerly a design consultant for Rowan and Jaeger Hand Knits and a freelance designer for Rowan Yarns, Carol now sells her own exclusive line of knitted bags and accessories. She also runs HK in Edinburgh, a store devoted to handknitting and knitted textiles. Carol's fresh, exciting designs have been featured in many magazines, and she has written several books. She lives in Glasgow, Scotland. Carol's projects are:

- *Loop'n'link bracelet, page 70*
- *Twister bracelet, page 71*
- *Organic bracelet, pages 82–83*
- *Delicate beaded bracelet, page 84*
- *Dangle earrings, page 101*
- *Flutterby pin, pages 108–109*
- *Fancy feather pin, page 113*
- *Spotty rings, pages 118–119*

Luise Roberts

Luise worked as a book designer before starting to write on a broad range of craft subjects. Luise was taught to knit and sew at an early age by her mother and exhibited as an embroiderer before enthusiastically turning her attention back to knit and crochet. Luise has written several books with the aim of making techniques more accessible, showing that there is a difference between a task being difficult and it being time-consuming, and that a little time spent can be very rewarding. She lives in London, England. Luise's projects are:

- *Denim watch straps, pages 76–78*
- *Daisy watch strap, pages 88–89*
- *Denim earrings, pages 96–98*
- *Hemp disk pins, pages 114–115*
- *Beaded rings, pages 120–122*

INDEX